The Art and Science of Game Development: Theoretical Foundations and Practical Insights

Kameron Hussain and Frahaan Hussain

Published by Sonar Publishing, 2024.

While every precaution has been taken in the preparation of this book, the publisher assumes no responsibility for errors or omissions, or for damages resulting from the use of the information contained herein.

THE ART AND SCIENCE OF GAME DEVELOPMENT: THEORETICAL FOUNDATIONS AND PRACTICAL INSIGHTS

The art and science of game development

Theoretical Foundations and Practical Insights

FIRST EDITION

Contents

Preface

In the rapidly evolving world of digital entertainment, game development stands as a complex and multifaceted discipline that merges creativity with technology. This book, "The Complete Guide to Game Development," is designed to provide a comprehensive exploration of the various aspects of game creation, from theoretical foundations to practical applications. As the gaming industry continues to grow and diversify, understanding the underlying principles and methodologies becomes crucial for aspiring developers, seasoned professionals, and enthusiasts alike.

Our journey begins with an introduction to game development theory, setting the stage for the intricate dance between creativity and logic that defines this field. We then delve into the core principles of game design, where the elements of gameplay mechanics, narrative, aesthetics, and player psychology come together to create engaging and memorable experiences.

The following chapters explore the technical and economic dimensions of game development, examining how mechanics and dynamics shape gameplay, the influence of in-game economies, and the impact of monetization strategies. We also investigate the role of technology, from the evolution of development tools to the future trends that will shape the industry.

Understanding the diversity of game genres and their theoretical underpinnings is crucial for any developer. We discuss the nuances of various genres, from RPGs and strategy games to sports and puzzle games, and how they cater to different player preferences.

Player interaction and social gaming are pivotal in today's connected world, and we address the design and community management strategies that foster vibrant player communities. Level design and world-building are given their due importance, highlighting the principles that create immersive and navigable game worlds.

Narrative plays a vital role in many games, and our exploration of the narrative paradigm delves into storytelling techniques, interactive narratives, and the unique challenges of writing for games. Sound and music, often the unsung heroes of game design, are also covered in detail, emphasizing their role in creating audio-visual harmony and enhancing player immersion.

Artificial intelligence (AI) is another critical aspect, with chapters dedicated to basic and advanced AI techniques, ethical considerations, and the future of AI-driven game design. User interface (UI) and user experience (UX) design are essential for ensuring intuitive and enjoyable player interactions, and we provide insights into best practices and innovative approaches in this area.

No game is complete without rigorous testing and quality assurance. We outline the importance of testing, various methods and techniques, and the role of feedback in refining gameplay. The business side of game development, from industry overview to marketing and selling games, is also thoroughly examined, offering practical advice for navigating the competitive landscape.

Games are powerful cultural artifacts, and we explore their cultural impact, educational potential, and the importance of cultural sensitivity in design. Ethical game design, another crucial topic, addresses responsible representation, addiction, and the ethical considerations that developers must navigate.

Criticism and analysis are vital for growth and improvement, and we discuss the role of reviews, academic approaches, and the balance between artistic vision and player expectations. Team dynamics and leadership are key to successful game development, and we provide strategies for building and leading effective teams.

Innovation is the lifeblood of the gaming industry, and we highlight the need for breaking conventional norms, leveraging new technologies, and pushing narrative boundaries. Finally, we look to the future, discussing emerging trends, the next generation of developers, and the evolving role of VR and AR in gaming.

This book aims to be a comprehensive resource for anyone interested in the multifaceted world of game development. Whether you are an aspiring developer, a seasoned professional, or simply a gaming enthusiast, we hope that this guide provides valuable insights, practical knowledge, and inspiration for your journey in the exciting world of game creation.

Chapter 1: Introduction to Game Development Theory

Overview of Game Development

Game development is a multifaceted process that encompasses the creation, design, programming, and release of video games. It involves a combination of creative and technical skills, requiring developers to not only conceptualize and design game elements but also implement and test them to ensure a seamless and engaging player experience.

At its core, game development is about creating interactive experiences that entertain, challenge, and sometimes educate players. This process starts with an idea or concept, which is then fleshed out into a detailed game design document. This document serves as a blueprint, outlining the game's mechanics, story, characters, art style, and more.

The development team typically includes various roles such as game designers, programmers, artists, sound designers, and testers. Each member brings a unique set of skills to the table, contributing to the overall vision and execution of the game. Collaboration and communication are key, as the team must work together to bring the game from concept to reality.

Game development can be broadly categorized into pre-production, production, and post-production phases. During pre-production, the team focuses on planning and conceptualizing the game. This phase involves creating prototypes, defining the game's scope, and setting goals and milestones. Production is where the actual development takes place, including coding, creating assets, and building the game world. Post-production involves testing, debugging, and polishing the game, followed by marketing and distribution.

The gaming industry has evolved significantly over the years, driven by advancements in technology and changing player preferences. From early arcade games to modern AAA titles and indie games, the landscape of game development is constantly shifting. Developers must stay abreast of the latest trends and technologies to create innovative and compelling experiences.

The success of a game often hinges on its ability to engage players. This involves a deep understanding of player psychology and the elements that make games enjoyable. Developers must consider factors such as challenge, reward, progression, and immersion when designing gameplay mechanics. Balancing these elements is crucial to creating a game that is both fun and rewarding to play.

In addition to entertainment, games have the potential to impact players on a deeper level. They can convey stories, evoke emotions, and even address social and cultural issues. As such, game developers have a responsibility to consider the broader implications of their work and strive for ethical and inclusive design practices.

The advent of new technologies such as virtual reality (VR), augmented reality (AR), and artificial intelligence (AI) is opening up new possibilities for game development. These technologies allow for more immersive and interactive experiences, pushing the boundaries of what is possible in gaming. Developers must be willing to experiment and innovate to stay ahead in this dynamic industry.

Indie game development has also seen a surge in popularity, with smaller teams and individual developers creating unique and innovative games. The rise of digital distribution platforms and crowdfunding has made it easier for indie developers to bring their games to market and reach a global audience.

Ultimately, game development is a blend of art and science. It requires creativity, technical expertise, and a deep understanding of player behavior. Whether working on a small indie project or a large-scale commercial game, developers must navigate numerous challenges and make countless decisions to bring their vision to life.

As we explore the various aspects of game development in this book, we will delve deeper into the theories, principles, and practicalities that underpin this fascinating field. From game design and mechanics to technology and business considerations, we aim to provide a comprehensive guide to the art and science of creating engaging and impactful games.

The Importance of Theory in Game Creation

Theory in game development serves as the foundation upon which practical applications are built. Understanding the theoretical principles behind game design and development enables creators to make informed decisions, innovate effectively, and create games that resonate with players on multiple levels. Theoretical knowledge provides a framework for analyzing and solving complex problems that arise during the game development process.

One of the primary reasons theory is important in game creation is that it offers a structured approach to understanding what makes games engaging and enjoyable. By studying established theories in areas such as psychology, narrative, and design, developers can identify the elements that contribute to a compelling game experience. This understanding helps in crafting mechanics, narratives, and visuals that align with players' expectations and preferences.

Game theory also plays a crucial role in balancing gameplay. Understanding concepts such as game balance, difficulty curves, and reward systems allows developers to create experiences that are challenging yet fair. A well-balanced game keeps players engaged by providing just the right level of challenge, avoiding frustration from overly difficult sections or boredom from overly easy ones.

Narrative theory is another critical aspect of game creation. Games often rely on storytelling to immerse players in their worlds and drive the gameplay experience. By applying principles from literary and cinematic theory, game writers and designers can construct narratives that are emotionally engaging and thematically rich. Techniques such as character development, plot structure, and pacing are essential tools in creating compelling stories within games.

Aesthetics theory helps developers understand the impact of visual and auditory elements on the player experience. Concepts such as color theory, composition, and sound design contribute to creating immersive and visually appealing game worlds. Aesthetic considerations also play a significant role in establishing the game's tone and atmosphere, enhancing the overall player experience.

Player psychology is another area where theory is invaluable. Understanding how players think and behave allows developers to design games that cater to different player types and motivations. Theories of player engagement, motivation, and satisfaction provide insights into what drives players to keep playing and how to create experiences that are both enjoyable and rewarding.

Economic theory can also be applied to game development, particularly in the context of in-game economies and monetization strategies. Understanding principles such as supply and demand, value perception, and consumer behavior helps developers design virtual economies that feel realistic and balanced. This knowledge is especially important in free-to-play games, where effective monetization strategies are crucial for the game's financial success.

The ethical implications of game design are another important consideration. Theories related to ethics and social responsibility guide developers in making decisions that promote inclusivity, diversity, and positive social impact. This includes considerations such as avoiding harmful stereotypes, ensuring fair representation, and designing games that are accessible to a wide range of players.

In addition to providing a foundation for practical design decisions, theory also fosters innovation. By understanding and challenging existing theories, developers can push the boundaries of what is possible in game design. Theoretical knowledge enables developers to experiment with new mechanics, narratives, and technologies, leading to the creation of unique and groundbreaking games.

As the gaming industry continues to evolve, the importance of theory in game creation will only grow. The rapid advancement of technology and changing player expectations require developers to constantly adapt and innovate. A strong theoretical foundation equips developers with the tools and knowledge needed to navigate these changes and continue creating engaging and impactful games.

In this book, we will explore various theoretical concepts and their practical applications in game development. From game design principles and mechanics to player psychology and narrative theory, each chapter will provide insights into the foundational knowledge that underpins successful game creation. By understanding and applying these theories, developers can enhance their craft and create games that stand the test of time.

Historical Perspectives on Game Development

The history of game development is a rich tapestry that reflects the evolution of technology, culture, and creativity. From the early days of arcade games to the sophisticated, immersive experiences of today, understanding the historical context of game development provides valuable insights into how the industry has grown and where it is headed.

The origins of video games can be traced back to the mid-20th century, with early experiments in computer technology. One of the first known video games, "Tennis for Two," was created in 1958 by physicist William Higinbotham. This simple game simulated a tennis match on an oscilloscope, laying the groundwork for future developments in interactive entertainment.

The 1970s marked the beginning of the commercial video game industry with the release of arcade games like "Pong" by Atari. "Pong" was a significant milestone, as it demonstrated the commercial viability of video games and sparked the growth of the arcade gaming culture. The success of arcade games led to the establishment of video game companies and the development of home consoles, such as the Atari 2600.

The 1980s saw rapid advancements in game technology and design. The introduction of more powerful home computers and gaming consoles allowed for more complex and visually appealing games. Iconic titles such as "Pac-Man," "Space Invaders," and "Super Mario Bros." became cultural phenomena, influencing a generation of gamers and developers. This era also saw the rise of game genres, including platformers, shooters, and role-playing games (RPGs).

The 1990s brought significant technological innovations, including the transition from 2D to 3D graphics. Games like "Doom," "Quake," and "Super Mario 64" showcased the potential of 3D environments, revolutionizing gameplay and design. The advent of CD-ROM technology also allowed for larger game worlds, better graphics, and more immersive soundtracks. This decade witnessed the rise of influential game developers and studios, shaping the future of the industry.

The early 2000s continued the trend of technological advancement with the introduction of more powerful gaming consoles, such as the PlayStation 2, Xbox, and Nintendo GameCube. Online gaming also gained popularity, enabling players to connect and compete with others around the world. Games like "World of Warcraft" and "Halo 2" demonstrated the potential of online multiplayer experiences, creating dedicated communities and expanding the social aspect of gaming.

In recent years, the gaming industry has continued to evolve, driven by advancements in hardware, software, and connectivity. The rise of mobile gaming has made games more accessible to a broader audience, with titles like "Angry Birds" and "Candy Crush Saga" becoming household names. The growth of indie game development has also introduced new and innovative game experiences, challenging traditional industry norms and expanding the diversity of available games.

The emergence of virtual reality (VR) and augmented reality (AR) technologies has opened up new possibilities for immersive gaming experiences. Games like "Beat Saber" and "Pokémon GO" showcase the potential of these technologies to create unique and engaging gameplay. The integration of AI and machine learning is also transforming game development, enabling more responsive and intelligent game worlds.

Understanding the historical perspectives on game development helps developers appreciate the roots of the industry and the technological and cultural shifts that have shaped it. This knowledge provides context for current trends and future innovations, guiding developers in creating games that build on past successes while pushing the boundaries of what is possible.

As we continue to explore the various aspects of game development in this book, we will draw on historical examples to illustrate key concepts and principles. By examining the evolution of game development, we can gain a deeper understanding of the challenges and opportunities that lie ahead. This historical perspective serves as a foundation for the theoretical and practical insights that will inform and inspire your journey in game creation.

Key Theoretical Concepts

Game development is a complex field that draws on a variety of theoretical concepts from different disciplines. These theories provide a framework for understanding and designing games, helping developers create engaging and meaningful experiences. In this section, we will explore some of the key theoretical concepts that underpin game development.

1. Game Design Theory

Game design theory focuses on the principles and practices of creating games. It encompasses a wide range of topics, including game mechanics, dynamics, aesthetics, and player experience. Understanding game design theory helps developers create balanced and engaging gameplay. Concepts such as flow, pacing, and feedback loops are central to designing games that keep players engaged and motivated.

2. Narrative Theory

Narrative theory examines the structure and elements of storytelling. In the context of game development, it explores how narratives can be integrated into gameplay to create immersive and emotionally engaging experiences. Key concepts include plot, character development, pacing, and branching narratives. Understanding narrative theory helps developers craft compelling stories that resonate with players and enhance the overall game experience.

3. Player Psychology

Player psychology explores the cognitive and emotional aspects of player behavior. This includes understanding what motivates players, how they learn, and how they experience emotions while playing games. Theories of motivation, such as self-determination theory and operant conditioning, provide insights into how to design reward systems and challenges that keep players engaged. Player psychology also informs accessibility and usability considerations, ensuring that games are enjoyable for a diverse audience.

4. Aesthetics Theory

Aesthetics theory examines the visual and auditory elements of games. It explores how design choices in art, sound, and music contribute to the overall player experience. Concepts such as color theory, composition, and sound design are essential for creating immersive and visually appealing game worlds. Aesthetics theory also considers the impact of art style on the game's tone and atmosphere.

5. Economic Theory

Economic theory is particularly relevant in the context of in-game economies and monetization strategies. It explores principles such as supply and demand, value perception, and consumer behavior. Understanding economic theory helps developers design virtual economies that are realistic and balanced, enhancing player engagement and satisfaction. This knowledge is also crucial for implementing effective monetization strategies, especially in free-to-play games.

6. Systems Theory

Systems theory examines the interrelationships and interactions between different elements of a game. It focuses on understanding how changes in one part of the system can affect the whole. This is particularly important in game design, where mechanics, dynamics, and aesthetics are interconnected. Systems theory provides tools for analyzing and optimizing these interactions to create cohesive and engaging gameplay experiences.

7. Ethical Theory

Ethical theory addresses the moral considerations involved in game development. This includes issues such as representation, inclusivity, and the potential impact of games on players and society. Ethical theory provides a framework for making responsible design choices that promote positive social impact and avoid harm. This is increasingly important as games become more influential and reach a broader audience.

8. Educational Theory

Educational theory explores how games can be used as tools for learning and education. Concepts such as scaffolding, experiential learning, and gamification are central to designing educational games that are both effective and engaging. Understanding educational theory helps developers create games that teach skills, convey knowledge, and foster critical thinking.

9. Interaction Design Theory

Interaction design theory focuses on the design of user interfaces and interactions within games. It explores how players interact with game elements and how these interactions can be designed to be intuitive and enjoyable. Key concepts include affordances, feedback, and usability. Interaction design theory is crucial for creating seamless and satisfying player experiences.

10. Cultural Theory

Cultural theory examines the role of games as cultural artifacts and their impact on society. It explores how games reflect and influence cultural norms, values, and identities. Understanding cultural theory helps developers create games that are culturally sensitive and resonate with diverse audiences. It also provides insights into how games can be used to address social issues and promote cultural understanding.

By understanding and applying these key theoretical concepts, developers can create games that are not only entertaining but also meaningful and impactful. These theories provide a foundation for making informed design decisions, solving complex problems, and pushing the boundaries of what is possible in game development.

The Structure of This Book

This book is structured to provide a comprehensive guide to game development, covering both theoretical foundations and practical applications. Each chapter is designed to build on the previous ones, offering a cohesive and detailed exploration of the various aspects of creating games. Here's an overview of the structure and content of this book.

Chapter 1: Introduction to Game Development Theory

In this chapter, we introduce the field of game development and discuss the importance of theoretical knowledge. We explore the historical perspectives of game development, key theoretical concepts, and provide an overview of the book's structure.

Chapter 2: Game Design Principles

This chapter delves into the core elements of game design. We discuss the principles of balancing gameplay mechanics, narrative and storytelling, aesthetics, and player psychology. These foundational concepts are essential for creating engaging and well-designed games.

Chapter 3: Mechanics and Dynamics

Here, we focus on the technical aspects of game mechanics and dynamics. We define game mechanics, explore how they are brought to life through dynamics, and examine case studies of successful mechanics. We also discuss the importance of balancing for different player types.

Chapter 4: Game Economics

This chapter explores the application of economic theories to gaming. We discuss in-game economies, virtual goods, monetization strategies, and the impact of economics on game design. Ethical considerations in game monetization are also covered.

Chapter 5: Technology in Game Development

We examine the evolution of game development technologies and current tech trends in gaming. This chapter covers choosing the right technology stack, the impact of hardware on game design, and future technologies that will shape the industry.

Chapter 6: Game Genres and Their Theories

This chapter defines different game genres and explores their theoretical underpinnings. We discuss RPGs, strategy games, sports and simulation games, and puzzles and casual games. Each genre is examined through its unique theoretical lens.

Chapter 7: Player Interaction and Social Gaming

We explore the theory of player interaction and the design of multiplayer experiences. This chapter covers social dynamics in games, community management, and player retention strategies. Case studies of successful community building are also included.

Chapter 8: Level Design and World Building

This chapter delves into the principles of level design and creating immersive game worlds. We discuss spatial theories, player navigation, environmental storytelling, and challenges in modern level design.

Chapter 9: The Narrative Paradigm

We focus on storytelling in games, exploring narrative structures, archetypes, and interactive narratives. This chapter also covers the challenges and techniques of writing for games, with case studies of games with strong narratives.

Chapter 10: Sound and Music in Games

This chapter examines the role of sound and music in game design. We discuss composing music for games, sound effects, audio immersion, and interactive audio. The future of audio in games is also explored.

Chapter 11: AI in Games

We cover the basics of game AI and advanced AI techniques. This chapter discusses AI-driven game design, player interaction, ethical issues, and the future of AI in game development.

Chapter 12: User Interface and User Experience

This chapter focuses on principles of game UI/UX design. We discuss designing intuitive interfaces, enhancing player experience, and UI/UX challenges in modern games. Case studies of UI/UX innovations are included.

Chapter 13: Testing and Quality Assurance

We explore the importance of game testing, methods and techniques, balancing gameplay, and handling feedback. This chapter includes case studies of testing leading to successful game launches.

Chapter 14: The Business of Game Development

This chapter provides an overview of the game industry, starting a game development business, funding and investment, marketing, and selling games. Navigating the challenges of the game industry is also discussed.

Chapter 15: Cultural Impact of Games

We examine games as cultural artifacts, their cultural influence, and their role in education and training. This chapter also covers the globalization of game culture and addressing cultural sensitivity in games.

Chapter 16: Ethical Game Design

This chapter discusses ethics in game development, responsible representation, designing games with a purpose, and addressing addiction and game usage. Ethical considerations in game content are also explored.

Chapter 17: The Role of Criticism and Analysis

We cover game reviews, academic approaches to game studies, the importance of feedback loops, and balancing artistic vision with player expectations. Learning from criticism is also discussed.

Chapter 18: Game Development Teams and Leadership

This chapter focuses on structuring a game development team, leadership, collaboration strategies, handling conflicts, and building a successful game development culture.

Chapter 19: Innovation in Game Development

We discuss the need for innovation in games, breaking conventional design norms, innovative use of technology, and pushing narrative boundaries. Future trends and opportunities in game design are also explored.

Chapter 20: The Future of Game Development

This chapter examines emerging trends and technologies, the next generation of game developers, predictions for the future game market, the role of VR and AR, and preparing for the evolving game industry.

By following this structured approach, readers will gain a comprehensive understanding of game development, from foundational theories to practical applications. Each chapter builds on the previous ones, providing a cohesive and detailed guide to the art and science of creating games.

Chapter 2: Game Design Principles

Core Elements of Game Design

Game design is the process of creating the content and rules of a game, including the gameplay mechanics, story, characters, and environment. Understanding the core elements of game design is essential for creating engaging and memorable experiences. These elements include gameplay mechanics, narrative, aesthetics, and player psychology.

Gameplay Mechanics

Gameplay mechanics are the rules and systems that define how a game operates and how players interact with it. These mechanics form the backbone of the game experience, dictating everything from character movement and combat to puzzle-solving and resource management. Effective game mechanics should be intuitive, challenging, and rewarding, providing players with clear goals and a sense of progression.

One of the key principles in designing gameplay mechanics is balance. A well-balanced game ensures that players face appropriate challenges and rewards, maintaining their engagement and motivation. This involves careful tuning of difficulty levels, resource availability, and the pacing of rewards and penalties.

Narrative

Narrative is the storytelling aspect of a game, encompassing the plot, characters, and world-building. A compelling narrative can significantly enhance the player's immersion and emotional connection to the game. It provides context and meaning to the gameplay mechanics, making the player's actions feel purposeful and impactful.

There are various ways to integrate narrative into a game, from linear storylines to branching paths and open-world exploration. The choice of narrative structure depends on the game's genre, target audience, and overall design goals. Interactive narratives, where player choices influence the story's outcome, can provide a deeper level of engagement and replayability.

Aesthetics

Aesthetics refer to the visual, auditory, and overall sensory elements of a game. This includes art style, sound design, music, and user interface. Aesthetics play a crucial role in setting the tone and atmosphere of a game, enhancing its emotional impact and immersion.

The choice of art style should align with the game's theme and narrative, whether it's realistic, cartoonish, minimalist, or abstract. Sound design and music also contribute to the game's atmosphere, creating tension, excitement, or relaxation as needed. The user interface should be intuitive and unobtrusive, allowing players to focus on the gameplay without unnecessary distractions.

Player Psychology

Understanding player psychology is essential for designing games that are engaging and enjoyable. This involves studying how players think, feel, and behave in response to different game elements. Key psychological concepts in game design include motivation, flow, and immersion.

Motivation refers to what drives players to engage with the game. This can include intrinsic motivations, such as the desire for mastery and exploration, and extrinsic motivations, such as rewards and achievements. Designing games that cater to different types of motivation can enhance player engagement and satisfaction.

Flow is the state of being fully immersed and focused on the game. Achieving flow requires a balance between challenge and skill, where the player is neither bored nor frustrated. Game designers can facilitate flow by providing clear goals, immediate feedback, and a gradual increase in difficulty.

Immersion is the sense of being absorbed in the game world. This can be achieved through a combination of compelling narrative, realistic visuals, and dynamic sound. The more immersive a game is, the more likely players are to lose track of time and become deeply engaged in the experience.

Interactivity

Interactivity is a defining feature of games, distinguishing them from other forms of media. It refers to the ability of players to influence and be influenced by the game world. This can include direct interactions, such as controlling a character or solving a puzzle, as well as indirect interactions, such as managing resources or making strategic decisions.

The level of interactivity in a game can vary widely, from simple point-and-click mechanics to complex simulations. Effective interactivity should provide players with meaningful choices and consequences, allowing them to shape their own experience and feel a sense of agency.

Replayability

Replayability is the potential for a game to be played multiple times without losing its appeal. This can be achieved through various design elements, such as multiple endings, randomized content, and procedurally generated levels. High replayability encourages players to return to the game, extending its lifespan and increasing its value.

Accessibility

Accessibility refers to designing games that can be enjoyed by a wide range of players, including those with disabilities. This can involve providing customizable controls, subtitles, colorblind modes, and other features that accommodate different needs. Ensuring accessibility not only makes games more inclusive but also broadens their potential audience.

By understanding and applying these core elements of game design, developers can create games that are engaging, enjoyable, and memorable. Each element plays a crucial role in shaping the overall player experience, contributing to the success and impact of the game.

Balancing Gameplay Mechanics

Balancing gameplay mechanics is a critical aspect of game design, ensuring that the game remains engaging, fair, and challenging for players. A well-balanced game provides a satisfying experience, where players feel a sense of achievement and progression without becoming frustrated or bored. Achieving this balance requires careful consideration of various factors, including difficulty, pacing, resource management, and player feedback.

Difficulty Levels

One of the primary aspects of balancing gameplay mechanics is adjusting the difficulty levels. A game should be challenging enough to keep players engaged but not so difficult that it becomes frustrating. This involves tuning the game's enemies, obstacles, puzzles, and other challenges to provide an appropriate level of difficulty for the target audience.

Dynamic difficulty adjustment (DDA) is a technique used to balance difficulty in real-time. It involves monitoring the player's performance and adjusting the game's difficulty accordingly. For example, if a player is struggling, the game might reduce the number of enemies or provide additional health packs. Conversely, if the player is performing well, the game might introduce tougher challenges to maintain engagement.

Pacing

Pacing refers to the rhythm and flow of the game, including the distribution of challenges, rewards, and narrative elements. Proper pacing ensures that players remain engaged and motivated throughout the game. This involves balancing periods of intense action with moments of relaxation and exploration.

Effective pacing requires careful planning of the game's levels, missions, and story beats. Designers should consider the player's emotional journey, providing moments of tension, excitement, and relief. The pacing should gradually increase in intensity, building towards climactic moments and then providing resolution.

Resource Management

Resource management is another crucial aspect of balancing gameplay mechanics. This includes managing in-game resources such as health, ammunition, currency, and items. Proper resource management ensures that players have enough resources to progress without making the game too easy or difficult.

Designers should carefully control the availability and distribution of resources, creating a sense of scarcity and reward. For example, players might need to explore and complete challenges to obtain valuable resources. Balancing resource management involves ensuring that players can acquire the necessary resources while maintaining a sense of challenge and strategy.

Player Feedback

Player feedback is essential for balancing gameplay mechanics. This includes both direct feedback from playtesting and indirect feedback from observing player behavior. Playtesting involves having players play the game and provide feedback on their experience, including the difficulty, pacing, and overall enjoyment.

Observing player behavior involves analyzing how players interact with the game, including where they struggle, succeed, and disengage. This data can provide valuable insights into how the game's mechanics are functioning and where adjustments are needed. Iterative testing and feedback are crucial for fine-tuning the game's balance.

Fairness and Challenge

Fairness is a key consideration in balancing gameplay mechanics. Players should feel that the game's challenges are fair and that their success is based on skill and strategy rather than luck or unfair advantages. This involves ensuring that the game provides clear rules, predictable outcomes, and reasonable challenges.

Designers should avoid creating situations where players feel punished unfairly or face insurmountable obstacles. Instead, challenges should be designed to test the player's abilities and provide a sense of accomplishment upon overcoming them. Fairness also involves providing appropriate rewards for the player's efforts, reinforcing their sense of progression and achievement.

Player Types and Preferences

Different players have different preferences and playstyles, and balancing gameplay mechanics involves catering to these diverse needs. This includes considering different player types, such as explorers, achievers, socializers, and killers, each of whom engages with games in different ways.

Providing multiple difficulty levels, customizable settings, and various gameplay options can help accommodate different player preferences. For example, some players might enjoy a challenging combat experience, while others prefer exploration and puzzle-solving. Balancing the game for different player types involves creating a flexible and inclusive design.

Examples of Balanced Gameplay

Examining successful games can provide valuable insights into effective gameplay balancing. For example, "The Legend of Zelda: Breath of the Wild" is known for its well-balanced mechanics, providing a vast open world with a variety of challenges and rewards. The game allows players to approach challenges in multiple ways, catering to different playstyles and preferences.

Another example is "Dark Souls," which is praised for its challenging but fair gameplay. The game's difficulty is balanced by providing players with clear rules, predictable enemy patterns, and opportunities to learn from their mistakes. This creates a sense of mastery and achievement as players progress.

By understanding and applying these principles of balancing gameplay mechanics, developers can create games that are engaging, fair, and challenging. Balancing is an iterative process that requires careful planning, testing, and feedback to ensure a satisfying and enjoyable player experience.

Narrative and Storytelling in Games

Narrative and storytelling play a crucial role in many games, providing context, meaning, and emotional engagement for players. A well-crafted narrative can transform a game from a simple collection of mechanics into a rich and immersive experience. In this section, we explore the key elements of narrative and storytelling in games, including plot, character development, pacing, and interactive narratives.

Plot

The plot is the sequence of events that make up the story of the game. It provides the framework for the narrative, guiding the player's journey and driving the gameplay forward. A compelling plot should have a clear beginning, middle, and end, with well-defined goals and obstacles for the player to overcome.

There are various types of plot structures that can be used in games, from linear narratives to branching storylines and open-world exploration. The choice of plot structure depends on the game's genre, target audience, and overall design goals. Linear narratives provide a focused and directed experience, while branching storylines and open-world exploration offer greater player agency and replayability.

Character Development

Characters are central to the narrative of a game, providing the human element that players can relate to and invest in. Well-developed characters have distinct personalities, motivations, and arcs, allowing players to connect with them on an emotional level. Character development involves creating believable and relatable characters, providing them with meaningful goals and challenges, and allowing them to grow and change over the course of the game.

In addition to the protagonist, supporting characters and antagonists play important roles in the narrative. Supporting characters can provide assistance, information, and emotional support, while antagonists create conflict and drive the plot forward. Each character should have a clear role and purpose in the story, contributing to the overall narrative and player experience.

Pacing

Pacing refers to the rhythm and flow of the narrative, including the distribution of story events, challenges, and rewards. Proper pacing ensures that players remain engaged and motivated throughout the game, providing a balanced mix of tension, excitement, and resolution. This involves carefully planning the timing and sequence of story events, as well as the intensity and variety of challenges.

Effective pacing requires a deep understanding of the player's emotional journey, providing moments of tension, excitement, and relief. The pacing should gradually build towards climactic moments, creating a sense of anticipation and satisfaction. This involves balancing periods of intense action with moments of relaxation and exploration, allowing players to catch their breath and absorb the story.

Interactive Narratives

Interactive narratives allow players to influence the story through their choices and actions. This can include branching storylines, multiple endings, and dynamic character interactions. Interactive narratives provide a deeper level of engagement and replayability, allowing players to shape their own experience and feel a sense of agency.

Designing interactive narratives requires careful planning and consideration of the possible paths and outcomes. Each choice should have meaningful consequences, affecting the story, characters, and gameplay. This involves creating a complex web of interconnected events and outcomes, ensuring that each path is coherent and satisfying.

Dialogue and Writing

Dialogue and writing are crucial elements of storytelling in games, providing the means for characters to communicate and express themselves. Well-written dialogue should be natural, engaging, and reflective of the character's personality and motivations. It should also serve to advance the plot, reveal character traits, and provide information to the player.

Writing for games involves unique challenges, including the need to accommodate player choices and interactions. This requires creating dialogue that can adapt to different situations and outcomes, providing a seamless and immersive experience. Effective writing also involves creating compelling and memorable lines, adding depth and personality to the characters and story.

Environmental Storytelling

Environmental storytelling is the use of the game environment to convey narrative elements and create a sense of place. This can include visual details, ambient sounds, and interactive objects that provide clues and context to the story. Environmental storytelling allows players to discover and interpret the narrative through exploration and observation, creating a more immersive and engaging experience.

Examples of environmental storytelling include hidden notes, audio logs, and visual details that hint at past events and character backstories. These elements can add depth and richness to the game world, providing a sense of history and continuity. Effective environmental storytelling involves careful attention to detail and a deep understanding of the game's lore and setting.

Emotional Engagement

Emotional engagement is a key aspect of narrative and storytelling in games, creating a deeper connection between the player and the game. This involves evoking emotions such as excitement, fear, joy, and sadness through the story, characters, and gameplay. Emotional engagement can enhance the player's investment in the game, making the experience more memorable and impactful.

Techniques for creating emotional engagement include using relatable characters, compelling conflicts, and meaningful choices. Music and sound design also play a crucial role in evoking emotions, creating tension, excitement, and atmosphere. By carefully crafting the narrative and emotional elements, developers can create a powerful and immersive experience for players.

Examples of Effective Storytelling

Examining successful games can provide valuable insights into effective storytelling techniques. For example, "The Last of Us" is known for its compelling narrative and well-developed characters, creating a deeply emotional and immersive experience. The game's plot, pacing, and character interactions are carefully crafted to evoke a range of emotions and keep players engaged.

Another example is "The Witcher 3: Wild Hunt," which features a rich and complex narrative with branching storylines and dynamic character interactions. The game's interactive narrative allows players to shape the story through their choices, creating a sense of agency and replayability. The writing, dialogue, and environmental storytelling are also highly praised, adding depth and richness to the game world.

By understanding and applying these principles of narrative and storytelling, developers can create games that are engaging, memorable, and emotionally impactful. The narrative elements play a crucial role in shaping the overall player experience, contributing to the success and impact of the game.

The Role of Aesthetics and Visuals

Aesthetics and visuals play a crucial role in game design, shaping the player's first impression and overall experience. The visual elements of a game include art style, color palette, character design, environments, and user interface. These elements work together to create an immersive and engaging world that enhances the gameplay and narrative. In this section, we explore the importance of aesthetics and visuals in game design and how they contribute to the overall player experience.

Art Style

The art style of a game defines its visual identity and sets the tone for the entire experience. It encompasses the overall look and feel of the game, including character designs, environments, and user interface. The choice of art style should align with the game's theme, narrative, and target audience.

There are various art styles that developers can choose from, including realistic, cartoonish, minimalist, and abstract. Each style has its unique strengths and can evoke different emotions and atmospheres. For example, a realistic art style can create a sense of immersion and believability, while a cartoonish style can add humor and lightheartedness.

Color Palette

The color palette is an essential aspect of a game's visual design, influencing the mood and atmosphere of the game world. Different colors can evoke different emotions and create various visual effects. For example, warm colors like red and orange can create a sense of excitement and urgency, while cool colors like blue and green can evoke calmness and tranquility.

Choosing the right color palette involves considering the game's theme, narrative, and art style. It should enhance the overall visual experience and contribute to the game's atmosphere. Color theory can provide valuable insights into how different colors interact and how to create harmonious and visually appealing palettes.

Character Design

Character design is a critical component of a game's visuals, influencing how players perceive and relate to the characters. Well-designed characters should be visually distinct, expressive, and reflective of their personality and role in the story. This involves creating unique silhouettes, facial expressions, and animations that convey the character's traits and emotions.

Character design also involves considering the practical aspects of gameplay, such as visibility and readability. Characters should be easily recognizable and distinguishable from the background and other elements. This is particularly important in fast-paced action games, where players need to quickly identify characters and their actions.

Environment Design

The design of the game environment plays a significant role in creating an immersive and believable world. This includes the layout, architecture, and visual details of the game world, as well as the use of lighting, shadows, and effects. A well-designed environment should provide a sense of place and context, enhancing the narrative and gameplay.

Environmental design involves creating visually appealing and functional spaces that guide the player's exploration and interaction. This includes designing levels, landscapes, and interiors that are both aesthetically pleasing and strategically designed for gameplay. The use of visual storytelling elements, such as props, signage, and environmental details, can add depth and context to the game world.

User Interface

The user interface (UI) is the means by which players interact with the game, including menus, HUDs (heads-up displays), and control systems. A well-designed UI should be intuitive, accessible, and visually consistent with the game's overall design. It should provide clear and concise information to the player without overwhelming or distracting them.

UI design involves considering the player's needs and preferences, ensuring that the interface is easy to navigate and use. This includes designing buttons, icons, and menus that are visually distinct and responsive. The use of visual cues, such as highlights, animations, and feedback, can enhance the usability and interactivity of the UI.

Visual Consistency

Visual consistency is essential for creating a cohesive and immersive game experience. This involves ensuring that all visual elements, from characters and environments to UI and effects, adhere to a unified art style and design principles. Consistency in visuals helps create a believable and engaging game world, allowing players to focus on the gameplay and narrative.

Maintaining visual consistency requires careful planning and coordination among the development team. This includes creating style guides, reference materials, and design documents that outline the visual direction and standards for the game. Regular reviews and feedback sessions can help ensure that all visual elements align with the overall design vision.

Emotional Impact

Aesthetics and visuals have a significant impact on the player's emotions and immersion. Visual elements can evoke a wide range of emotions, from excitement and fear to joy and sadness. By carefully crafting the visual experience, developers can enhance the emotional engagement and overall impact of the game.

Techniques for creating emotional impact include the use of color, lighting, composition, and animation. For example, dramatic lighting and shadows can create tension and suspense, while bright and vibrant colors can evoke happiness and energy. Dynamic and expressive animations can bring characters to life, making them more relatable and engaging.

Examples of Effective Visual Design

Examining successful games can provide valuable insights into effective visual design techniques. For example, "Journey" is known for its stunning visuals and minimalist art style, creating a serene and meditative experience. The use of color, lighting, and fluid animations enhances the emotional impact and sense of exploration.

Another example is "Hollow Knight," which features a distinct and cohesive visual style with hand-drawn art and detailed environments. The game's use of color, lighting, and animation creates a dark and atmospheric world, enhancing the sense of mystery and adventure.

By understanding and applying these principles of aesthetics and visual design, developers can create games that are visually engaging, immersive, and emotionally impactful. The visual elements play a crucial role in shaping the overall player experience, contributing to the success and impact of the game.

Player Psychology and Engagement

Player psychology is a critical aspect of game design, focusing on understanding how players think, feel, and behave. By understanding player psychology, developers can create games that are engaging, enjoyable, and satisfying. This section explores key psychological concepts in game design, including motivation, flow, immersion, and player types.

Motivation

Motivation is what drives players to engage with a game. Understanding what motivates players can help designers create experiences that keep them engaged and satisfied. There are two main types of motivation: intrinsic and extrinsic.

Intrinsic motivation comes from within the player and is driven by personal satisfaction and enjoyment. Players who are intrinsically motivated play games for the fun and challenge they provide. They enjoy mastering skills, solving puzzles, and exploring game worlds.

Extrinsic motivation comes from external rewards, such as points, achievements, and in-game currency. Players who are extrinsically motivated are driven by the desire to earn rewards and recognition. They are motivated by the tangible benefits and incentives provided by the game.

Effective game design caters to both intrinsic and extrinsic motivations, providing a balance of challenges, rewards, and goals. This involves designing gameplay mechanics, challenges, and rewards that appeal to different player motivations and preferences.

Flow

Flow is the state of being fully immersed and focused on the game. Achieving flow is a key goal of game design, as it leads to a highly enjoyable and engaging experience. Flow occurs when players are fully absorbed in the game, losing track of time and feeling a sense of control and mastery.

To achieve flow, game designers must balance the difficulty of the game with the player's skill level. The game should provide clear goals, immediate feedback, and a gradual increase in difficulty. When the challenge is too high, players may feel frustrated, while when the challenge is too low, they may feel bored. The optimal experience lies in the middle, where players are continually challenged but able to succeed.

Immersion

Immersion is the sense of being absorbed and transported into the game world. Immersive games create a sense of presence, where players feel like they are part of the game environment. Immersion is achieved through a combination of compelling narrative, realistic visuals, dynamic sound, and interactive gameplay.

Techniques for creating immersion include detailed world-building, engaging storylines, and realistic character interactions. The use of visual and auditory cues, such as ambient sounds, lighting, and weather effects, can enhance the sense of immersion. Providing players with meaningful choices and consequences also contributes to immersion, as it allows them to shape their own experience and feel a sense of agency.

Player Types

Different players have different preferences and playstyles, and understanding these player types can help designers create games that cater to a diverse audience. One popular model for categorizing player types is the Bartle taxonomy, which identifies four main types: achievers, explorers, socializers, and killers.

Achievers are motivated by the desire to complete goals and earn rewards. They enjoy challenges, achievements, and progressing through the game. Achievers are driven by extrinsic rewards and the satisfaction of mastery.

Explorers are motivated by the desire to discover and explore the game world. They enjoy uncovering secrets, solving puzzles, and learning about the game's lore. Explorers are driven by intrinsic rewards and the joy of discovery.

Socializers are motivated by the desire to interact with other players. They enjoy forming relationships, collaborating, and participating in social activities. Socializers are driven by the social aspects of the game and the sense of community.

Killers are motivated by the desire to compete and dominate other players. They enjoy PvP (player versus player) combat, competition, and asserting their power. Killers are driven by the thrill of competition and the satisfaction of victory.

By understanding these player types, designers can create games that offer a variety of experiences and cater to different preferences. This involves providing a mix of challenges, exploration opportunities, social interactions, and competitive gameplay.

Rewards and Feedback

Rewards and feedback are essential for keeping players engaged and motivated. Rewards provide a sense of accomplishment and progression, while feedback helps players understand their actions and make informed decisions. Effective use of rewards and feedback involves balancing extrinsic and intrinsic rewards, providing clear and immediate feedback, and designing meaningful and satisfying rewards.

Extrinsic rewards include points, achievements, and in-game currency, while intrinsic rewards include the satisfaction of mastering a skill, solving a puzzle, or completing a challenge. Providing a mix of both types of rewards can enhance player engagement and motivation.

Clear and immediate feedback is essential for helping players understand their actions and progress. This includes visual and auditory cues, such as sound effects, animations, and notifications, as well as more detailed feedback, such as progress bars, scoreboards, and performance summaries.

Emotional Engagement

Emotional engagement is a key aspect of player psychology, creating a deeper connection between the player and the game. Games can evoke a wide range of emotions, from excitement and joy to fear and sadness. By carefully crafting the emotional elements of the game, designers can enhance the overall player experience and create a more memorable and impactful game.

Techniques for creating emotional engagement include using relatable characters, compelling conflicts, and meaningful choices. Music and sound design also play a crucial role in evoking emotions, creating tension, excitement, and atmosphere. By understanding and applying these principles, developers can create games that resonate with players on an emotional level.

Examples of Engaging Games

Examining successful games can provide valuable insights into effective player engagement techniques. For example, "Celeste" is known for its challenging gameplay and emotional narrative. The game provides clear goals, immediate feedback, and a gradual increase in difficulty, creating a satisfying flow experience. The narrative and characters also evoke a range of emotions, enhancing the overall engagement.

Another example is "Animal Crossing: New Horizons," which appeals to a wide range of player types with its mix of exploration, social interaction, and customization. The game provides intrinsic rewards through the joy of discovery and extrinsic rewards through achievements and in-game currency. The relaxing pace and charming visuals create a highly immersive and engaging experience.

By understanding and applying these principles of player psychology and engagement, developers can create games that are enjoyable, satisfying, and memorable. These psychological concepts play a crucial role in shaping the overall player experience, contributing to the success and impact of the game.

Chapter 3: Mechanics and Dynamics

Defining Game Mechanics

Game mechanics are the rules and systems that dictate how a game operates. They are the fundamental building blocks that guide player interactions and the overall game experience. Understanding game mechanics is crucial for creating engaging and balanced gameplay.

Game mechanics can be categorized into several types, including core mechanics, primary mechanics, and secondary mechanics. Core mechanics are the essential actions players take repeatedly throughout the game, such as jumping in a platformer or shooting in a first-person shooter. Primary mechanics support the core mechanics and add depth to the gameplay, like power-ups or special abilities. Secondary mechanics are additional features that enhance the overall experience but are not central to the gameplay, such as scoring systems or collectible items.

An example of a core mechanic is the movement system in "Super Mario Bros." The ability to run, jump, and navigate levels is fundamental to the game's design. Primary mechanics in this game include power-ups like the Super Mushroom and Fire Flower, which provide additional abilities and strategic options. Secondary mechanics might include the collection of coins and the scoring system that rewards players for their performance.

Implementing mechanics effectively requires a balance between simplicity and complexity. Simple mechanics are easy to understand and use, while complex mechanics can add depth and replayability. However, overly complex mechanics can overwhelm players and detract from the overall experience. Therefore, designers must carefully consider how mechanics interact and support each other.

In designing game mechanics, it's essential to consider player feedback and iteration. Playtesting is a critical process where designers observe how players interact with the mechanics and gather feedback to refine and improve the gameplay. Iterative design ensures that mechanics are intuitive, enjoyable, and provide the desired level of challenge.

Another important aspect of game mechanics is their consistency. Mechanics should behave predictably and follow logical rules to avoid confusing players. Consistency helps players learn and master the game, leading to a more satisfying experience.

Game mechanics also need to align with the game's theme and narrative. Mechanics should support the story and setting, creating a cohesive experience. For example, in a stealth game, mechanics like hiding, sneaking, and disguising should be emphasized to reinforce the theme of espionage and secrecy.

Balancing game mechanics is a complex task that involves adjusting variables and testing different configurations to ensure fair and engaging gameplay. Balance affects the difficulty curve, the distribution of rewards and penalties, and the pacing of the game. A well-balanced game keeps players engaged without causing frustration or boredom.

In summary, game mechanics are the backbone of any game, defining how players interact with the game world and each other. Effective mechanics are well-designed, balanced, and aligned with the game's theme, providing a satisfying and engaging experience for players. Through playtesting and iteration, designers can refine mechanics to achieve the desired gameplay experience.

Dynamics: Bringing Mechanics to Life

Game dynamics refer to the emergent behavior and interactions that arise from the implementation of game mechanics. While mechanics are the rules and systems, dynamics are the outcomes and experiences that result from these rules in action. Understanding game dynamics is essential for creating engaging and immersive gameplay.

Dynamics are shaped by the player's actions and decisions, as well as the interactions between different mechanics. For example, in a strategy game, the mechanics of resource management, unit movement, and combat come together to create dynamic gameplay where players must make strategic decisions, adapt to changing situations, and outmaneuver their opponents.

One key aspect of game dynamics is the concept of emergence. Emergent gameplay occurs when simple mechanics interact in complex ways, leading to unexpected and often delightful outcomes. This can create a sense of discovery and excitement for players, as they explore the possibilities within the game. A classic example of emergent gameplay is the "sandbox" style of games like "Minecraft," where players can combine simple actions like mining and crafting to create intricate structures and systems.

Player agency is another crucial factor in game dynamics. Agency refers to the player's ability to make meaningful choices that impact the game world. High levels of agency can lead to more engaging and personalized experiences, as players feel that their decisions matter. Game designers can enhance agency by providing multiple pathways, strategies, and outcomes based on player choices.

Feedback loops are an important dynamic that can influence player behavior and the overall game experience. Positive feedback loops reinforce a player's actions, often leading to exponential growth or success. Negative feedback loops, on the other hand, counterbalance player actions to maintain equilibrium and prevent runaway success. For example, in a racing game, a positive feedback loop might reward the player with speed boosts for successful maneuvers, while a negative feedback loop might implement rubber-banding to keep races competitive.

Tension and release are dynamic elements that can create emotional engagement and a sense of pacing in a game. By introducing challenges and obstacles, designers can build tension, which is then released when the player overcomes these hurdles. This dynamic can create a satisfying rhythm of challenge and reward, keeping players invested in the game.

Social dynamics also play a significant role in multiplayer games. The interactions between players, such as cooperation, competition, and communication, can create rich and varied gameplay experiences. Social dynamics are influenced by the game's mechanics, such as team-based objectives, leaderboards, and in-game communication tools. Designing for positive social dynamics can enhance player retention and create strong communities around the game.

Balancing game dynamics involves fine-tuning the interactions between mechanics to achieve the desired gameplay experience. This requires extensive playtesting and analysis to identify and address any issues that arise. Designers must consider how different player types and playstyles will interact with the game dynamics and make adjustments to ensure a balanced and enjoyable experience for all players.

In conclusion, game dynamics bring mechanics to life by creating the emergent behavior and interactions that define the player's experience. By understanding and designing for dynamics such as emergence, player agency, feedback loops, tension and release, and social interactions, designers can create engaging and immersive gameplay that keeps players coming back for more.

Complexity and Depth in Game Mechanics

Complexity and depth are crucial elements in game mechanics that contribute to the overall richness and engagement of a game. While they are often used interchangeably, they refer to different aspects of game design. Complexity involves the number of rules, systems, and interactions within a game, whereas depth refers to the meaningful choices and strategies that emerge from these elements.

Achieving the right balance of complexity and depth is essential for creating a game that is both accessible and challenging. A game that is too complex can overwhelm players with too many rules and systems to manage. Conversely, a game that lacks depth can become boring and repetitive, as players quickly exhaust the strategic possibilities.

One way to manage complexity is through modular design, where the game is divided into distinct systems or modules that can be learned and mastered individually. For example, a strategy game might have separate modules for resource management, unit combat, and diplomacy. By introducing these systems gradually, players can build their understanding and proficiency without feeling overwhelmed.

Depth, on the other hand, is achieved by ensuring that the game mechanics offer meaningful choices and strategic options. This can be accomplished through emergent gameplay, where simple mechanics interact in complex ways to create a wide range of possibilities. Games like "Chess" and "Go" are classic examples of depth, where a few simple rules lead to a vast array of strategies and tactics.

Designers can also create depth by encouraging player creativity and experimentation. Sandbox games, for instance, provide players with tools and mechanics that can be used in various ways, allowing them to discover new strategies and solutions. This kind of player-driven exploration can lead to highly engaging and replayable experiences.

Balancing complexity and depth involves careful consideration of the game's learning curve. The learning curve should be designed to gradually introduce players to new mechanics and concepts, allowing them to build their skills and understanding over time. Tutorials, tooltips, and gradual difficulty progression can help ease players into more complex and deep gameplay.

Another important factor is player feedback. By observing how players interact with the game and gathering feedback, designers can identify areas where the complexity might be too high or the depth insufficient. Iterative design and playtesting are crucial for fine-tuning these elements and ensuring a balanced and enjoyable experience.

In some cases, designers might choose to simplify certain aspects of the game to reduce unnecessary complexity while maintaining depth. This can involve streamlining interfaces, automating repetitive tasks, or removing redundant mechanics. The goal is to create a game that is easy to learn but hard to master, offering both immediate accessibility and long-term engagement.

Balancing different player types and preferences is also essential. Some players enjoy mastering complex systems and deep strategies, while others prefer more straightforward and casual experiences. Offering multiple difficulty levels, customizable settings, or different game modes can help cater to a diverse audience.

In conclusion, complexity and depth are vital components of game mechanics that contribute to a game's richness and engagement. By balancing these elements through modular design, emergent gameplay, player creativity, and iterative feedback, designers can create games that are both accessible and challenging, providing a rewarding experience for a wide range of players.

Case Studies of Successful Mechanics

Examining case studies of successful game mechanics can provide valuable insights into the principles and practices that lead to engaging and memorable gameplay. These case studies highlight how innovative and well-implemented mechanics can elevate a game and contribute to its success.

Case Study 1: "The Legend of Zelda: Breath of the Wild"

One of the most acclaimed games in recent years, "The Legend of Zelda: Breath of the Wild," is renowned for its open-world design and innovative mechanics. The game features a variety of mechanics that contribute to its depth and replayability, such as the physics-based interaction system, the stamina meter, and the cooking system.

The physics-based interaction system allows players to manipulate the environment in creative ways. For example, players can cut down trees to create bridges, use metal objects to conduct electricity, and exploit the game's weather system to gain advantages. This mechanic encourages experimentation and rewards player creativity, leading to emergent gameplay.

The stamina meter adds a layer of strategy to exploration and combat. Players must manage their stamina when climbing, swimming, or performing special attacks. This mechanic creates tension and forces players to plan their actions carefully, adding depth to the gameplay.

The cooking system allows players to gather ingredients and create meals that provide various buffs and benefits. This mechanic encourages exploration and resource management, as players seek out rare ingredients and experiment with different recipes. The cooking system also adds a layer of personalization, as players can tailor their meals to suit their playstyle and needs.

Case Study 2: "Dark Souls"

"Dark Souls" is another game that is often cited for its innovative mechanics and challenging gameplay. The game's combat system, bonfire checkpoint mechanic, and online multiplayer integration are key elements that contribute to its depth and engagement.

The combat system in "Dark Souls" is known for its precision and complexity. Players must carefully time their attacks, blocks, and dodges, with even small mistakes leading to significant consequences. This mechanic rewards skill and mastery, creating a satisfying and rewarding experience for dedicated players.

The bonfire checkpoint mechanic serves as both a save point and a respawn location. When players rest at a bonfire, enemies respawn, creating a risk-reward dynamic. Players must decide when to rest and reset their progress, adding a strategic layer to the gameplay.

The online multiplayer integration allows players to interact with each other in unique ways. Players can leave messages for others, summon allies for cooperative play, or invade other players' worlds for PvP combat. This mechanic creates a dynamic and interconnected game world, where player actions can have far-reaching impacts.

Case Study 3: "Minecraft"

"Minecraft" is a prime example of a game with simple mechanics that lead to deep and emergent gameplay. The core mechanics of mining, crafting, and building provide a foundation for limitless creativity and exploration.

Mining and crafting are the central mechanics of "Minecraft." Players gather resources from the environment and use them to create tools, structures, and other items. This mechanic encourages exploration and resource management, as players must seek out rare materials and plan their crafting projects.

The building mechanic allows players to create structures and environments with almost complete freedom. This mechanic fosters creativity and self-expression, as players can design and build anything they can imagine. The sandbox nature of "Minecraft" means that the game is as deep and engaging as the player's creativity allows.

Conclusion

These case studies demonstrate how well-designed mechanics can elevate a game and contribute to its success. By focusing on innovation, player creativity, and strategic depth, designers can create engaging and memorable gameplay experiences. Examining successful mechanics can provide valuable insights and inspiration for game developers looking to create their own compelling mechanics.

Balancing for Different Player Types

Balancing a game to cater to different player types is a crucial aspect of game design. Players have varied preferences, playstyles, and skill levels, and a well-balanced game ensures that all players can have a satisfying experience. Understanding player types and designing mechanics that accommodate them is key to achieving this balance.

One common framework for categorizing player types is the Bartle taxonomy, which identifies four primary types: Achievers, Explorers, Socializers, and Killers. Each type has distinct motivations and preferences, and balancing for these types involves providing content and mechanics that appeal to each.

Achievers

Achievers are motivated by completing goals, earning rewards, and achieving high scores. To balance a game for Achievers, designers should include clear objectives, challenging tasks, and a robust system of rewards and achievements. Leaderboards, progression systems, and in-game achievements can provide the motivation and recognition that Achievers seek.

Explorers

Explorers enjoy discovering new areas, uncovering secrets, and learning about the game world. For Explorers, designers should focus on creating rich, detailed environments with hidden content and lore. Mechanics that encourage exploration, such as open-world design, collectibles, and hidden quests, can keep Explorers engaged and satisfied.

Socializers

Socializers are motivated by interacting with other players and forming social connections. To cater to Socializers, designers should include mechanics that facilitate communication and cooperation. Multiplayer modes, guild systems, and in-game chat can create opportunities for social interaction. Events and activities that require teamwork and collaboration can also appeal to this player type.

Killers

Killers thrive on competition and dominance over other players. For Killers, competitive gameplay modes, such as PvP combat, leaderboards, and tournaments, can provide the excitement and challenge they seek. Balancing for Killers involves ensuring that competitive mechanics are fair and rewarding skill and strategy.

Balancing Strategies

Balancing for different player types requires a holistic approach that considers the interplay between various mechanics and systems. Here are some strategies for achieving balance:

1. **Modular Design**: Implement modular systems that can cater to different player types. For example, a game might include separate progression tracks for PvP and PvE content, allowing players to choose their preferred playstyle.
2. **Difficulty Levels**: Offer multiple difficulty levels to accommodate different skill levels. This allows players to choose a level of challenge

that suits their preferences and abilities.

3. **Customization**: Provide options for players to customize their experience. This can include character customization, skill trees, and adjustable game settings. Customization allows players to tailor the game to their playstyle.

4. **Feedback and Iteration**: Gather feedback from a diverse player base and use it to inform balance adjustments. Playtesting with different player types can reveal imbalances and areas for improvement. Iterative design ensures that the game evolves to meet player needs.

5. **Dynamic Systems**: Implement dynamic systems that adapt to player behavior. For example, an AI director that adjusts difficulty based on player performance can help maintain balance and challenge.

6. **Content Variety**: Include a variety of content that appeals to different player types. This can involve offering different game modes, activities, and challenges. Variety ensures that all players have something to engage with.

In conclusion, balancing a game for different player types involves understanding their motivations and designing mechanics that cater to their preferences. By using strategies such as modular design, difficulty levels, customization, feedback, dynamic systems, and content variety, designers can create a balanced and enjoyable experience for all players.

Chapter 4: Game Economics

Economic Theories Applied to Gaming

Economic theories provide valuable insights into the design and operation of in-game economies. By applying principles from microeconomics and macroeconomics, game designers can create systems that simulate real-world economic behavior and enhance player engagement.

Microeconomics in Gaming

Microeconomics focuses on the behavior of individuals and firms, and how they make decisions regarding the allocation of resources. In games, microeconomic principles can be applied to create systems where players make choices about resource management, production, and consumption.

One key concept in microeconomics is supply and demand. In a game economy, the supply of resources or items can be controlled through mechanics such as crafting, farming, or loot drops. Demand is driven by player needs and preferences, which can be influenced by the utility and scarcity of items. Balancing supply and demand is crucial for maintaining a stable economy and preventing issues such as inflation or resource hoarding.

Another important principle is opportunity cost, which refers to the value of the next best alternative foregone when making a decision. In games, players often face choices about how to allocate their time and resources. For example, they might choose between spending time gathering resources or completing quests. Designing mechanics that make players consider opportunity costs can add depth and strategic complexity to the game.

Macroeconomics in Gaming

Macroeconomics deals with the behavior of economies as a whole, including issues such as inflation, unemployment, and economic growth. In-game economies can simulate macroeconomic principles to create dynamic and immersive experiences.

Inflation can occur in a game economy when the supply of currency or valuable items increases faster than the demand. This can lead to a decrease in the value of money and an increase in prices. Designers can implement mechanisms to control inflation, such as sinks that remove currency from the economy (e.g., repair costs, taxes, or expensive luxury items).

Economic growth in a game can be represented by the expansion of player capabilities, resources, and territories. Mechanics that encourage investment, such as building infrastructure or upgrading equipment, can simulate economic growth and create a sense of progress and development.

Behavioral Economics

Behavioral economics studies how psychological factors influence economic decision-making. In games, understanding player behavior and motivations can help designers create more engaging and rewarding economic systems.

For example, the concept of loss aversion, where people prefer avoiding losses over acquiring equivalent gains, can be used to design risk-reward mechanics. Players might be more motivated to protect their resources or investments if they perceive a significant risk of loss.

The endowment effect, where people ascribe more value to things they own, can influence how players interact with in-game items and assets. By allowing players to customize and personalize their possessions, designers can increase the perceived value and attachment to these items.

Virtual Goods and Real-World Economics

Virtual goods, such as skins, mounts, or in-game currency, have become a significant aspect of many game economies. The sale and trade of virtual goods can mimic real-world economic behavior and create complex market dynamics.

The secondary market for virtual goods, where players buy and sell items for real money, introduces real-world economic considerations. Designers must be aware of issues such as market regulation, fraud prevention, and the impact on gameplay balance. Ensuring fair and secure transactions is crucial for maintaining player trust and a healthy economy.

Ethical Considerations

The design of in-game economies also raises ethical considerations. Issues such as pay-to-win mechanics, where players can gain competitive advantages through purchases, can lead to imbalances and player dissatisfaction. Designers must balance monetization strategies with fair gameplay to avoid alienating players.

Loot boxes and other randomized reward systems have come under scrutiny for their potential to encourage gambling-like behavior. Transparency and regulation are essential to ensure that these mechanics are ethical and do not exploit players.

In conclusion, applying economic theories to game design can create more realistic and engaging in-game economies. By understanding principles from microeconomics, macroeconomics, and behavioral economics, designers can create systems that simulate real-world economic behavior and enhance player engagement. Ethical considerations are also crucial to ensure that these systems are fair and responsible.

In-game Economies and Virtual Goods

In-game economies and virtual goods have become central to modern game design, offering players additional layers of engagement and providing developers with monetization opportunities. Understanding how to create and manage these economies is crucial for ensuring a balanced and enjoyable player experience.

Designing In-game Economies

In-game economies simulate real-world economic systems, providing players with opportunities to earn, spend, and trade virtual goods. A well-designed economy adds depth to gameplay and can significantly enhance player retention and satisfaction.

The foundation of an in-game economy is its currency system. Currencies can take various forms, such as gold, credits, or gems, and are used for transactions within the game. Designers must decide how players earn and spend currency, balancing the rate of acquisition with meaningful expenditure opportunities. Common methods for earning currency include completing quests, defeating enemies, and selling items.

Virtual Goods

Virtual goods are items that players can acquire within the game, ranging from functional equipment to purely cosmetic enhancements. These goods can be categorized into several types:

1. **Functional Items**: These include weapons, armor, and tools that impact gameplay. They often have attributes that enhance player performance, making them highly desirable.
2. **Consumables**: Items such as health potions, experience boosters, and crafting materials that are used and depleted. These goods drive continuous player engagement as they need to be replenished.
3. **Cosmetic Items**: Skins, outfits, and mounts that change the appearance of characters or objects without affecting gameplay. These items are popular for personalization and self-expression.
4. **Virtual Services**: These include character name changes, server transfers, and additional storage space. They offer convenience and customization options to players.

Monetization Strategies

Monetization in games often revolves around the sale of virtual goods. Effective strategies must balance revenue generation with maintaining a fair and enjoyable player experience.

1. **Microtransactions**: Small purchases of virtual goods or currency. This model is widely used in free-to-play games, allowing players to spend small amounts frequently.
2. **Premium Currency**: A special currency purchased with real money,

used to buy exclusive or high-value items. This creates a dual-currency system where one currency is earned through gameplay and the other through purchases.

3. **Loot Boxes**: Randomized rewards that players can buy or earn, containing a variety of virtual goods. While they can drive significant revenue, they also raise ethical concerns about gambling-like mechanics.

4. **Battle Passes**: A tiered system offering rewards for completing in-game challenges over a set period. Players can purchase a pass to unlock premium rewards while still earning free rewards through gameplay.

5. **Subscription Models**: Regular payments for ongoing access to premium content or benefits. This model provides steady revenue and can enhance player loyalty.

Balancing the Economy

Maintaining a balanced in-game economy is essential to avoid inflation, resource hoarding, and player frustration. Key considerations include:

1. **Resource Scarcity**: Ensuring that valuable items remain rare and require effort to obtain. This creates a sense of achievement and value.

2. **Sinks and Faucets**: Balancing currency generation (faucets) with ways to spend currency (sinks). Examples of sinks include repair costs, crafting fees, and exclusive items.

3. **Dynamic Pricing**: Adjusting prices based on supply and demand to prevent market saturation and maintain item value.

4. **Player Trading**: Allowing players to trade items and currency can create a vibrant player-driven economy. However, it requires robust systems to prevent fraud and ensure fair trading.

Ethical Considerations

Designing in-game economies also involves ethical considerations, particularly regarding monetization practices. Transparent communication about the value and odds of virtual goods is essential to maintain player trust. Avoiding pay-to-win mechanics, where players can buy competitive advantages, is crucial for fair play.

Regulatory scrutiny of loot boxes and similar mechanics has increased, prompting developers to adopt more transparent and ethical practices. Offering value without exploiting players ensures long-term success and a positive reputation.

In conclusion, in-game economies and virtual goods are integral to modern game design, offering engagement and monetization opportunities. By designing balanced economies, offering a variety of virtual goods, and implementing ethical monetization strategies, developers can create immersive and rewarding experiences for players.

Monetization Strategies

Monetization strategies are critical for the financial success of a game, particularly in the context of free-to-play models. Effective monetization balances revenue generation with player satisfaction, ensuring that the game's economic model enhances rather than detracts from the overall experience.

Free-to-Play (F2P) Model

The F2P model allows players to access the game for free while offering in-game purchases to generate revenue. This model relies on a large player base and a variety of monetization strategies to convert a percentage of players into paying customers.

Microtransactions

Microtransactions involve small, frequent purchases of virtual goods or currency. These can include cosmetic items, consumables, and convenience features. The key to successful microtransactions is offering desirable items that do not disrupt game balance. Players should feel that purchases enhance their experience without giving an unfair advantage.

Premium Currency

Premium currency is a virtual currency bought with real money, used to purchase exclusive or high-value items. This system allows players to buy premium currency in bulk and spend it gradually, creating a sense of progression and investment. Balancing the availability and pricing of premium currency is crucial to avoid alienating non-paying players.

Loot Boxes

Loot boxes offer randomized rewards and can be bought or earned through gameplay. While they can generate significant revenue, they also pose ethical concerns about gambling-like mechanics. Transparency about the odds of obtaining specific items and providing alternative ways to earn rewards can help mitigate these concerns.

Battle Passes

Battle passes provide a tiered reward system for completing in-game challenges over a set period. Players can purchase a pass to unlock premium rewards while still earning free rewards through gameplay. This model encourages regular play and offers a clear value proposition, enhancing player retention and engagement.

Subscription Models

Subscription models involve regular payments for ongoing access to premium content or benefits. This can include exclusive items, additional game modes, or enhanced features. Subscriptions provide a steady revenue stream and can enhance player loyalty by offering consistent value.

Advertising

In-game advertising can generate revenue without direct player spending. Ads can be integrated into the game in various ways, such as rewarded video ads, banner ads, or sponsored content. Rewarded ads, where players choose to watch an ad in exchange for in-game rewards, are particularly effective as they offer value without disrupting gameplay.

Event-Based Monetization

Special events, such as seasonal content or limited-time offers, can drive player spending by creating urgency and excitement. These events often feature exclusive items, discounts, and bonuses that encourage players to make purchases. Regularly updating the game with new events keeps the content fresh and maintains player interest.

Ethical Considerations

Ethical considerations are paramount in designing monetization strategies. Transparency about the cost and value of virtual goods, avoiding pay-to-win mechanics, and respecting player time and investment are crucial for maintaining player trust and satisfaction. Regulatory scrutiny of monetization practices, particularly loot boxes, necessitates adherence to ethical standards and responsible design.

Balancing Monetization and Player Experience

Balancing monetization with player experience involves offering value without disrupting gameplay. Key principles include:

1. **Fairness**: Ensuring that purchases do not provide unfair advantages or create a pay-to-win environment.
2. **Transparency**: Clearly communicating the cost, value, and odds of obtaining virtual goods.
3. **Player Choice**: Providing multiple ways for players to earn or purchase items, catering to different playstyles and preferences.
4. **Value Proposition**: Offering items and services that enhance the player experience and provide clear benefits.

Case Study: Successful Monetization

A successful example of ethical monetization is "Fortnite" by Epic Games. The game offers a free-to-play model with revenue generated through cosmetic items, battle passes, and event-based content. The premium currency (V-Bucks) is used to purchase skins, emotes, and other cosmetic enhancements. Importantly, these purchases do not impact gameplay balance, maintaining fairness for all players.

The battle pass system in "Fortnite" provides a clear value proposition, with players earning rewards through gameplay while also having the option to purchase the pass for additional exclusive content. Regular events and updates keep the game fresh, driving player engagement and spending.

In conclusion, effective monetization strategies balance revenue generation with player satisfaction. By employing microtransactions, premium currency, loot boxes, battle passes, subscriptions, advertising, and event-based content, developers can create a sustainable economic model. Ethical considerations and a focus on enhancing the player experience are essential for long-term success and player retention.

The Impact of Economics on Game Design

The economic systems within a game have a profound impact on its design, influencing everything from player behavior to narrative structure. Understanding and integrating economic principles into game design can lead to more engaging, balanced, and immersive experiences.

Player Motivation and Behavior

Economic systems can drive player motivation by providing goals, rewards, and progression. For example, a well-designed currency system can encourage players to complete quests, defeat enemies, or participate in events to earn rewards. This creates a loop of effort and reward that keeps players engaged.

The scarcity of resources plays a critical role in shaping player behavior. Scarce resources, whether they are in-game currency, crafting materials, or powerful items, can create a sense of urgency and value. Players are motivated to seek out these resources, trade with others, or invest time and effort into acquiring them.

Progression and Reward Systems

Economics is closely tied to progression systems, where players advance through the game by accumulating experience points, levels, and gear. A balanced progression system ensures that players feel a sense of achievement and growth without becoming overpowered too quickly.

Reward systems, such as loot drops, quest rewards, and achievement unlocks, rely on economic principles to determine the value and rarity of rewards. Designers must balance these systems to provide meaningful rewards that motivate players while maintaining the overall game balance.

Crafting and Trading Systems

Crafting systems allow players to create items using resources gathered in the game. These systems add depth and strategic planning, as players must decide how to allocate resources and which items to craft. Crafting also ties into the game's economy by creating demand for specific resources and items.

Trading systems enable players to exchange items and currency, creating a player-driven economy. This adds a social dimension to the game, as players interact and negotiate with each other. Designers must ensure that trading systems are secure and balanced to prevent exploitation and maintain fairness.

Game Balance and Inflation

Economic systems can impact game balance by influencing the availability and power of items, currency, and resources. Inflation, where the value of currency decreases due to oversupply, can destabilize the economy and devalue rewards. Designers can counteract inflation by introducing currency sinks, such as repair costs, taxes, or exclusive high-cost items.

Balancing the economy involves adjusting the rate at which players earn and spend resources. This includes setting appropriate prices for items, determining drop rates for loot, and designing sinks and faucets to regulate currency flow. A balanced economy ensures that players are consistently challenged and rewarded.

Narrative and World-Building

Economic systems can enhance the narrative and world-building aspects of a game. A well-designed economy can reflect the game's lore, culture, and setting. For example, a medieval fantasy game might feature a barter system, while a futuristic sci-fi game could use digital credits.

Integrating economic elements into the story can create a more immersive experience. Quests that involve trading, resource management, or economic conflict can add depth to the narrative. NPCs (non-player characters) with distinct economic roles, such as merchants, craftsmen, and traders, can enrich the game world and provide players with meaningful interactions.

Player Retention and Monetization

Economic systems play a crucial role in player retention and monetization. By providing ongoing goals and rewards, a well-designed economy keeps players engaged and encourages long-term play. Regular updates that introduce new items, resources, and economic challenges can maintain player interest.

Monetization strategies, such as microtransactions and premium currency, are closely tied to the game's economy. These systems must be carefully balanced to ensure that they provide value without disrupting gameplay. Fair and transparent monetization practices build player trust and contribute to the game's financial success.

Ethical Considerations

Designing economic systems also involves ethical considerations. Pay-to-win mechanics, where players can buy advantages with real money, can create imbalances and alienate non-paying players. Loot boxes and randomized rewards raise concerns about gambling-like behavior and transparency.

Designers must ensure that economic systems are fair, transparent, and respectful of players' time and investment. This includes clearly communicating the value of virtual goods, providing alternative ways to earn rewards, and avoiding exploitative practices.

In conclusion, the impact of economics on game design is multifaceted, influencing player motivation, progression, crafting, trading, balance, narrative, retention, and monetization. By understanding and integrating economic principles, designers can create more engaging, balanced, and immersive games. Ethical considerations are paramount to maintaining player trust and ensuring a positive experience.

Ethical Considerations in Game Monetization

The monetization of games, particularly in the free-to-play model, raises several ethical considerations that developers must navigate to ensure fair and responsible practices. Balancing revenue generation with player trust and satisfaction is crucial for long-term success.

Transparency and Disclosure

Transparency in monetization practices is essential to build and maintain player trust. Developers should clearly disclose the cost, value, and odds of obtaining virtual goods, particularly in the case of randomized rewards such as loot boxes. Providing this information helps players make informed decisions and reduces the perception of exploitative practices.

Fairness and Balance

Fairness in monetization involves ensuring that players who spend money do not gain an unfair advantage over those who do not. Pay-to-win mechanics, where paying players can purchase significant gameplay advantages, can create imbalances and frustrate non-paying players. Designers should strive to balance the game so that spending money enhances the experience without disrupting fair competition.

Avoiding Exploitative Practices

Monetization strategies should avoid exploiting players' psychological tendencies. This includes mechanisms that encourage excessive spending, such as time-limited offers, pressure to keep up with paying players, or manipulation of reward schedules to maximize spending. Ethical monetization respects players' time and financial investment, offering value without coercion.

Age Appropriateness

Many games appeal to a wide age range, including children and teenagers. Ethical monetization practices must consider the vulnerability of younger players. This includes avoiding aggressive marketing tactics, providing parental controls, and adhering to regulations that protect minors from exploitative practices. Age-appropriate content and spending limits can help ensure that games remain suitable for younger audiences.

Data Privacy and Security

Monetization systems often involve collecting and processing player data, including payment information. Ensuring the privacy and security of this data is paramount. Developers must implement robust security measures, comply with data protection regulations, and be transparent about how player data is used. Respecting players' privacy builds trust and safeguards their personal information.

Regulatory Compliance

As the game industry grows, it faces increasing regulatory scrutiny, particularly concerning monetization practices. Developers must stay informed about relevant laws and regulations, such as those governing loot boxes, gambling, and consumer protection. Compliance with these regulations is essential to avoid legal issues and maintain a positive reputation.

Providing Value and Satisfaction

Ultimately, ethical monetization is about providing value and satisfaction to players. This means offering virtual goods and services that enhance the gameplay experience, respecting players' time and investment, and ensuring that purchases feel rewarding. By focusing on player satisfaction, developers can create a positive relationship with their audience, fostering loyalty and long-term engagement.

Examples of Ethical Monetization

1. **Fortnite**: "Fortnite" by Epic Games offers a free-to-play model with revenue generated through cosmetic items and battle passes. The game's monetization practices are transparent, with clear pricing and no pay-to-win mechanics. This approach has earned player trust and contributed to the game's success.
2. **Warframe**: "Warframe" by Digital Extremes uses a free-to-play model with microtransactions for cosmetic items and convenience features. The game provides a fair balance between paying and non-paying players, with all gameplay content available for free. The developers maintain transparency and regularly communicate with the player community.
3. **Path of Exile**: "Path of Exile" by Grinding Gear Games offers a free-to-play model with microtransactions for cosmetic enhancements and additional storage space. The game's monetization is fair, with no impact on gameplay balance. The developers are transparent about their practices and engage with the community to address concerns.

Conclusion

Ethical considerations in game monetization are essential for maintaining player trust, satisfaction, and long-term success. By focusing on transparency, fairness, avoiding exploitative practices, age appropriateness, data privacy, regulatory compliance, and providing value, developers can create monetization systems that enhance the player experience while ensuring responsible practices. Ethical monetization not only benefits players but also contributes to a positive reputation and sustainable business model for developers.

Chapter 5: Technology in Game Development

Evolution of Game Development Technologies

Game development technologies have evolved significantly since the early days of video games. In the 1970s and 1980s, game development was limited by the hardware capabilities of early gaming consoles and personal computers. Games like "Pong" and "Space Invaders" were created with simple graphics and limited memory.

The 1990s saw a significant leap in technology with the advent of 16-bit and 32-bit consoles such as the Super Nintendo Entertainment System (SNES) and the Sony PlayStation. These systems allowed for more complex graphics, sound, and gameplay mechanics. The introduction of 3D graphics revolutionized the industry, with games like "Super Mario 64" setting new standards.

The early 2000s continued this trend with the release of more powerful consoles and the rise of PC gaming. Games became more realistic and immersive, thanks to advancements in graphics processing units (GPUs) and more sophisticated game engines. Middleware solutions, such as the Havok physics engine, allowed developers to create more dynamic and interactive environments.

In recent years, the game development landscape has been transformed by the rise of mobile gaming and the proliferation of smartphones. The introduction of powerful mobile processors has enabled developers to create console-quality games for mobile devices. Additionally, the advent of app stores has made it easier for indie developers to distribute their games.

Virtual reality (VR) and augmented reality (AR) are the latest frontiers in game development technology. VR headsets like the Oculus Rift and AR applications like Pokémon GO have opened up new possibilities for immersive gaming experiences. These technologies require specialized hardware and software, pushing the boundaries of what is possible in game development.

Cloud gaming is another emerging trend that promises to revolutionize the industry. Services like Google Stadia and NVIDIA GeForce Now allow players to stream games directly to their devices, eliminating the need for high-end hardware. This shift to cloud-based gaming could make gaming more accessible to a wider audience.

The use of artificial intelligence (AI) in game development has also seen significant advancements. AI is used to create more realistic non-player characters (NPCs) and to develop adaptive gameplay experiences that respond to the player's actions. Machine learning algorithms are being employed to optimize game performance and enhance procedural content generation.

Game engines have become more powerful and user-friendly, enabling developers to create high-quality games with fewer resources. Engines like Unity and Unreal Engine 4 offer comprehensive toolsets for 2D and 3D game development. These engines also support cross-platform development, allowing games to be deployed on multiple devices with minimal adjustments.

The evolution of game development technologies has been driven by both hardware and software innovations. As hardware becomes more powerful, software tools and engines evolve to take advantage of these advancements. This symbiotic relationship has led to the creation of increasingly complex and engaging games.

The rise of online multiplayer gaming has also had a significant impact on game development technologies. Developers must now consider network latency, server architecture, and data security when creating online games. Technologies such as peer-to-peer networking and dedicated servers are used to ensure smooth and secure online gameplay.

Game development has also become more collaborative, with teams often distributed across the globe. Tools like version control systems (e.g., Git) and project management software (e.g., JIRA) facilitate collaboration and ensure that team members can work together effectively, regardless of their location.

In summary, the evolution of game development technologies has been marked by continuous innovation and adaptation. From the early days of simple 2D games to the complex, immersive experiences of today, technology has been a driving force in the advancement of the gaming industry. As new technologies continue to emerge, the possibilities for game development are virtually limitless.

Current Tech Trends in Gaming

The gaming industry is continuously evolving, with new technologies and trends shaping the future of game development. One of the most significant current trends is the integration of artificial intelligence (AI) in various aspects of game design. AI is used to create more intelligent and responsive NPCs, develop adaptive gameplay that changes based on player behavior, and optimize game performance through machine learning algorithms.

Another major trend is the growing importance of virtual reality (VR) and augmented reality (AR). These technologies provide immersive experiences that transport players to entirely new worlds. VR headsets like the Oculus Rift and AR applications like Pokémon GO have gained popularity, prompting developers to explore new ways to incorporate these technologies into their games. The challenge lies in creating content that fully utilizes the potential of VR and AR while ensuring a seamless and comfortable user experience.

Cloud gaming is also gaining traction, offering players the ability to stream games directly to their devices without the need for high-end hardware. Services such as Google Stadia, NVIDIA GeForce Now, and Xbox Cloud Gaming are leading the charge in this area. Cloud gaming promises to make high-quality gaming experiences accessible to a broader audience, although it requires robust internet infrastructure to minimize latency and ensure smooth gameplay.

Blockchain technology and non-fungible tokens (NFTs) are emerging trends that are beginning to influence game development. Blockchain can provide secure and transparent ways to manage in-game assets, while NFTs allow for the creation of unique digital items that players can own, trade, or sell. This has the potential to create new economic models within games, though it also raises concerns about security, regulation, and environmental impact.

The rise of esports has also had a significant impact on game development. Competitive gaming requires a focus on balance, fairness, and performance optimization. Developers are now designing games with esports in mind, ensuring that they can support large-scale tournaments and provide features that enhance the viewing experience for spectators. This includes integrating streaming capabilities and developing tools for organizing and managing competitions.

Cross-platform play is becoming increasingly common, allowing players on different devices to compete and cooperate in the same game. This trend is driven by the desire to create inclusive gaming communities and remove barriers between players. Developers must ensure that their games perform well across various platforms, which can be challenging given the differences in hardware capabilities and control schemes.

Another trend is the focus on accessibility in game design. Developers are making concerted efforts to create games that can be enjoyed by a wider range of players, including those with disabilities. This includes implementing features such as customizable controls, subtitles, and colorblind modes. The goal is to ensure that everyone has the opportunity to enjoy gaming, regardless of their physical or cognitive abilities.

Social gaming experiences are also on the rise, with games incorporating social elements to enhance player engagement. This can include features like in-game chat, friend lists, and cooperative gameplay modes. Social interaction is a key driver of player retention, and developers are leveraging these elements to create more engaging and community-driven experiences.

The use of procedural generation in game development is another notable trend. Procedural generation algorithms can create vast and varied game worlds with minimal human intervention. This allows developers to produce content more efficiently and provides players with unique experiences each time they play. Games like "No Man's Sky" and "Minecraft" have demonstrated the potential of procedural generation to create expansive and dynamic environments.

Sustainability and environmental impact are becoming important considerations in game development. As the industry grows, developers are seeking ways to reduce their carbon footprint and promote sustainable practices. This includes optimizing game performance to reduce energy consumption and exploring eco-friendly distribution methods.

Finally, the integration of advanced physics and realistic animations is enhancing the realism of games. Developers are using sophisticated physics engines and motion capture technology to create more lifelike movements and interactions. This not only improves the visual appeal of games but also enhances the overall immersion and player experience.

In conclusion, the current tech trends in gaming are driving innovation and shaping the future of the industry. From AI and VR to blockchain and cloud gaming, these trends are creating new opportunities and challenges for developers. As technology continues to advance, the possibilities for game development will expand, leading to even more exciting and immersive gaming experiences.

Choosing the Right Technology Stack

Choosing the right technology stack is a critical decision in game development that can significantly impact the project's success. The technology stack encompasses the programming languages, frameworks, libraries, and tools used to create the game. Several factors must be considered when selecting a technology stack, including the target platform, game genre, team expertise, and project scope.

The first consideration is the target platform. Games can be developed for various platforms, including PC, consoles, mobile devices, and web browsers. Each platform has its own set of requirements and constraints. For example, mobile games may need to prioritize performance and battery efficiency, while PC and console games can leverage more powerful hardware. Cross-platform development is also an option, allowing the game to be released on multiple platforms with a single codebase.

Programming languages are a fundamental component of the technology stack. Common languages in game development include C++, C#, and JavaScript. C++ is widely used for its performance and control over low-level system resources, making it ideal for high-performance games. C# is popular for its ease of use and integration with the Unity engine, while JavaScript is often used for web-based games. The choice of language should align with the team's expertise and the specific needs of the project.

Game engines play a crucial role in the development process by providing a framework for building games. Popular game engines include Unity, Unreal Engine, and Godot. Unity is known for its versatility and support for 2D and 3D games across multiple platforms. Unreal Engine offers advanced graphics capabilities and is commonly used for AAA titles. Godot is an open-source engine that provides a flexible and lightweight solution for indie developers. Selecting the right engine depends on the game's requirements and the development team's familiarity with the tool.

Middleware solutions can enhance the development process by providing specialized functionality that would be time-consuming to develop from scratch. Examples include physics engines like Havok, audio middleware like FMOD, and animation tools like Spine. Middleware can streamline development and improve the quality of the final product, but it also adds complexity and potential licensing costs.

Version control systems are essential for managing the game's source code and assets. Tools like Git and Perforce allow multiple developers to collaborate on the project, track changes, and revert to previous versions if needed. Version control is particularly important for large teams and complex projects, as it helps maintain organization and prevent data loss.

Integrated development environments (IDEs) and text editors are also important components of the technology stack. IDEs like Visual Studio and JetBrains Rider provide a comprehensive suite of tools for coding, debugging, and testing. Text editors like Visual Studio Code offer a lightweight alternative with customizable features through extensions. The choice of IDE or text editor often comes down to personal preference and the specific needs of the project.

Testing and debugging tools are crucial for ensuring the game's quality and performance. Automated testing frameworks, such as NUnit and JUnit, can help identify bugs and verify that game mechanics function as intended. Profiling tools, like Unity Profiler and Unreal's built-in profiler, allow developers to analyze performance and optimize the game's efficiency.

Asset creation tools are used to develop the game's visual and audio content. Software like Adobe Photoshop, Blender, and Autodesk Maya are commonly used for creating 2D and 3D assets. Audio tools like Audacity and Ableton Live enable the production of sound effects and music. The choice of tools depends on the artistic direction of the game and the expertise of the development team.

Finally, project management tools are essential for planning, tracking, and coordinating the development process. Tools like JIRA, Trello, and Asana help manage tasks, milestones, and team collaboration. Effective project management ensures that the development stays on schedule and within budget, while also facilitating communication and coordination among team members.

In summary, choosing the right technology stack involves careful consideration of various factors, including the target platform, programming languages, game engines, middleware, version control systems, IDEs, testing tools, asset creation tools, and project management tools. By selecting the appropriate technologies, developers can streamline the development process, enhance the quality of the final product, and increase the likelihood of the project's success.

The Impact of Hardware on Game Design

Hardware plays a pivotal role in game design, influencing everything from graphics and performance to user experience and accessibility. The capabilities and limitations of hardware must be considered throughout the development process to ensure that the game meets technical requirements and delivers an optimal experience for players.

One of the primary considerations is the performance of the target hardware. High-performance hardware, such as gaming PCs and next-generation consoles, allows for advanced graphics, complex simulations, and large-scale environments. Developers can leverage powerful GPUs, high-speed CPUs, and ample memory to create visually stunning and immersive experiences. However, not all players have access to high-end hardware, so developers must also consider optimizing their games for lower-end systems to reach a broader audience.

Graphics are a critical aspect of game design that is heavily influenced by hardware capabilities. The resolution, frame rate, and level of detail achievable in a game depend on the power of the GPU. High-resolution textures, realistic lighting, and advanced shaders require significant processing power. Developers must balance graphical fidelity with performance to ensure that the game runs smoothly on the target hardware. Techniques such as level of detail (LOD) scaling, dynamic resolution, and texture streaming can help manage performance while maintaining visual quality.

Input devices are another important hardware consideration. Different platforms support various input methods, including keyboards, mice, game controllers, touchscreens, and motion sensors. Game design must account for these input methods to provide an intuitive and responsive user experience. For example, a first-person shooter on PC may use a mouse and keyboard for precise aiming, while a console version might be optimized for gamepad controls. Ensuring that the game is accessible and enjoyable across different input devices is crucial for reaching a diverse audience.

Storage limitations can also impact game design. While modern consoles and PCs often have substantial storage capacities, developers must still consider the size of game assets and how they are managed. Large games with high-resolution textures, detailed models, and extensive audio files can consume significant storage space. Efficient asset compression, streaming techniques, and content management systems are essential for optimizing storage usage and ensuring that the game can be installed and played without excessive delays.

Network capabilities are a critical factor for online and multiplayer games. The quality of the player's internet connection can affect gameplay, with issues such as latency, packet loss, and bandwidth limitations impacting the experience. Developers must design their games to handle varying network conditions, implementing features like lag compensation, predictive algorithms, and efficient data transmission protocols. Ensuring a smooth and enjoyable online experience requires careful consideration of network hardware and infrastructure.

Virtual reality (VR) and augmented reality (AR) present unique hardware challenges. VR headsets require high frame rates and low latency to provide a comfortable and immersive experience. AR applications must account for the capabilities of mobile devices and their cameras, sensors, and processing power. Designing for VR and AR involves optimizing performance, managing motion sickness, and creating intuitive interactions that take advantage of the hardware's features.

Audio hardware also influences game design. High-quality sound systems, surround sound, and advanced audio processing can enhance the immersive experience of a game. Developers can use spatial audio techniques to create realistic soundscapes that respond to the player's actions and environment. However, they must also ensure that the game sounds good on standard audio setups, including headphones and basic speakers.

Accessibility is another important consideration. Hardware capabilities can impact the ability of players with disabilities to enjoy the game. Developers should design their games with accessibility in mind, providing options for customizable controls, subtitles, colorblind modes, and other features that accommodate different needs. Ensuring that the game is playable on various hardware configurations can help make it more inclusive and accessible to a wider audience.

In conclusion, the impact of hardware on game design is multifaceted, affecting performance, graphics, input methods, storage, network capabilities, VR/AR experiences, audio, and accessibility. Developers must carefully consider the hardware limitations and capabilities of their target platforms to create games that deliver a high-quality experience for all players. By optimizing for different hardware configurations and leveraging advanced technologies, developers can create games that are both visually stunning and technically robust.

Future Technologies and Game Development

The future of game development is poised to be shaped by several emerging technologies that promise to revolutionize the way games are created, played, and experienced. These technologies include advancements in artificial intelligence (AI), virtual reality (VR) and augmented reality (AR), cloud gaming, blockchain, and more.

Artificial intelligence (AI) is expected to play an even more significant role in game development in the coming years. AI-driven game design will enable the creation of more complex and dynamic game worlds, with NPCs that exhibit realistic behaviors and adapt to the player's actions. Machine learning algorithms will be used to enhance procedural content generation, optimizing game performance and creating personalized experiences for players.

Virtual reality (VR) and augmented reality (AR) are set to become more mainstream, with improvements in hardware and software making these technologies more accessible and immersive. Future VR headsets will offer higher resolutions, wider fields of view, and better motion tracking, reducing motion sickness and enhancing the sense of presence. AR applications will benefit from advancements in mobile device capabilities, enabling more sophisticated and interactive experiences.

Cloud gaming is another technology that is expected to transform the industry. As internet infrastructure continues to improve, cloud gaming services will become more viable, allowing players to stream games directly to their devices without the need for high-end hardware. This will democratize access to high-quality gaming experiences and reduce the barrier to entry for players. Developers will need to design games that can leverage the benefits of cloud gaming while addressing challenges related to latency and data security.

Blockchain technology has the potential to revolutionize in-game economies and digital asset management. By using blockchain, developers can create secure and transparent systems for managing virtual goods, currencies, and NFTs. This could lead to new economic models within games, where players have true ownership of their in-game assets and can trade or sell them outside the game environment. However, the environmental impact and regulatory challenges of blockchain technology will need to be addressed.

The integration of haptic feedback and advanced sensory technologies will enhance the tactile and immersive aspects of gaming. Haptic gloves, suits, and other devices will allow players to feel textures, impacts, and movements within the game, creating a more immersive and interactive experience. These technologies will require careful design to ensure they complement gameplay and do not cause discomfort or fatigue.

5G technology is expected to significantly impact mobile gaming by providing faster and more reliable internet connections. This will enable more complex and data-intensive games to be played on mobile devices, with reduced latency and improved multiplayer experiences. Developers will be able to create more ambitious mobile games that take advantage of the increased bandwidth and low latency offered by 5G networks.

Advancements in graphics technology, such as ray tracing and real-time global illumination, will continue to push the boundaries of visual fidelity in games. These technologies will allow for more realistic lighting, reflections, and shadows, enhancing the overall immersion and aesthetic appeal of games. As GPUs become more powerful, developers will be able to incorporate these advanced graphics techniques into their games without compromising performance.

The rise of wearable technology, such as smartwatches and fitness trackers, will open up new possibilities for game development. These devices can be used to create games that incorporate physical activity and biometric data, offering unique and personalized gameplay experiences. For example, a game could adjust its difficulty based on the player's heart rate or encourage physical exercise as part of the gameplay.

Voice recognition and natural language processing (NLP) technologies will enable more intuitive and immersive interactions within games. Players will be able to use voice commands to control their characters, interact with NPCs, and navigate game menus. NLP will allow for more natural and dynamic conversations with NPCs, enhancing the storytelling and immersion of games.

Finally, quantum computing, though still in its early stages, has the potential to revolutionize game development by providing unprecedented computational power. Quantum computers could solve complex problems and simulations much faster than traditional computers, enabling the creation of more complex and detailed game worlds. While practical applications of quantum computing in game development are still a long way off, the potential is immense.

In conclusion, the future of game development will be shaped by a range of emerging technologies, including AI, VR/AR, cloud gaming, blockchain, haptic feedback, 5G, advanced graphics, wearable technology, voice recognition, and quantum computing. These technologies will enable developers to create more immersive, dynamic, and personalized gaming experiences. As the industry continues to evolve, staying at the forefront of these technological advancements will be crucial for developers looking to innovate and push the boundaries of what is possible in game development.

Chapter 6: Game Genres and Their Theories

Defining Different Game Genres

Game genres provide a framework for categorizing and understanding the vast array of video games available. They help players find games that align with their interests and preferences, and they guide developers in designing games that meet specific expectations. While the lines between genres can sometimes blur, several core categories are widely recognized in the gaming industry.

Action games are one of the most popular genres, characterized by fast-paced gameplay that requires quick reflexes and hand-eye coordination. These games often involve combat, platforming, and exploration. Examples include classic titles like "Super Mario Bros." and modern hits like "Fortnite." Action games can be further divided into subgenres such as platformers, shooters, and fighting games.

Adventure games focus on storytelling, exploration, and puzzle-solving. They often feature rich narratives and immersive worlds that players can explore at their own pace. Classic examples include "The Legend of Zelda" series and point-and-click adventures like "Monkey Island." Modern adventure games, such as "The Last of Us," blend action elements with deep storytelling.

Role-playing games (RPGs) are defined by their emphasis on character development, narrative, and exploration. Players typically assume the roles of characters in a fictional world, embarking on quests and making decisions that affect the story. RPGs can be divided into Western RPGs, like "The Elder Scrolls" series, and Japanese RPGs (JRPGs), like "Final Fantasy." Subgenres include action RPGs, tactical RPGs, and massively multiplayer online RPGs (MMORPGs).

Simulation games aim to replicate real-world activities and systems, providing players with a realistic or abstract representation of various experiences. This genre includes life simulations like "The Sims," vehicle simulations like "Flight

Simulator," and business simulations like "SimCity." Simulation games often emphasize management, strategy, and creativity.

Strategy games require players to plan and make decisions to achieve specific objectives. They can be divided into real-time strategy (RTS) games, where players must manage resources and units in real-time, and turn-based strategy (TBS) games, where players take turns making their moves. Notable examples include "StarCraft" (RTS) and "Civilization" (TBS). Strategy games often involve complex systems and require careful planning and foresight.

Sports games simulate the experience of playing various sports, such as soccer, basketball, and racing. These games can range from realistic simulations, like the "FIFA" series, to more arcade-style experiences, like "Mario Kart." Sports games often feature multiplayer modes, allowing players to compete against each other locally or online.

Puzzle games challenge players to solve problems and complete tasks using logic, pattern recognition, and strategic thinking. They can vary from simple match-three games like "Candy Crush" to complex brainteasers like "The Witness." Puzzle games often have a casual appeal, making them accessible to a wide audience.

Horror games are designed to evoke fear and tension in players. They often feature dark and unsettling environments, supernatural elements, and psychological horror. Classic examples include "Resident Evil" and "Silent Hill." Modern horror games, such as "Outlast," use advanced graphics and sound design to create immersive and terrifying experiences.

Sandbox games provide players with an open-ended environment where they can create, explore, and interact with the world at their own pace. These games often lack a defined structure or objectives, allowing players to set their own goals. "Minecraft" is a quintessential sandbox game, offering players the freedom to build and explore in a procedurally generated world.

Music and rhythm games challenge players to follow along with musical patterns and rhythms. These games often require precise timing and coordination. Examples include "Guitar Hero" and "Dance Dance Revolution."

Music games can be highly engaging and offer a unique gameplay experience centered around music and performance.

Educational games are designed to teach players new skills or knowledge through interactive experiences. They can cover a wide range of subjects, from math and science to history and language. Educational games often blend gameplay with learning objectives, making them a valuable tool for both entertainment and education.

In conclusion, game genres provide a useful framework for categorizing and understanding the diverse array of video games available. Each genre offers unique gameplay experiences and appeals to different player preferences. While the boundaries between genres can sometimes overlap, the core categories help guide players and developers in navigating the gaming landscape.

Theoretical Approaches to RPGs

Role-playing games (RPGs) are a diverse and complex genre that has evolved significantly over the years. The theoretical approaches to RPGs encompass various aspects, including narrative structure, character development, gameplay mechanics, and player agency. Understanding these theories can provide valuable insights into what makes RPGs engaging and immersive.

One of the fundamental theories in RPG design is the importance of narrative structure. RPGs are often defined by their rich and intricate storylines, which guide the player's journey through the game world. The narrative structure in RPGs can be linear, branching, or open-ended. Linear narratives offer a predefined path with a clear beginning, middle, and end, while branching narratives allow players to make choices that affect the outcome of the story. Open-ended narratives provide players with a sandbox environment where they can create their own stories.

Character development is another crucial aspect of RPGs. The theory of character progression involves designing systems that allow players to customize and evolve their characters over time. This can include leveling up, acquiring new skills and abilities, and finding or crafting better equipment.

Character development provides a sense of growth and achievement, motivating players to continue their journey.

Player agency is a central theoretical concept in RPGs, referring to the degree of control and influence players have over the game world and its narrative. High player agency allows for meaningful choices that can significantly impact the game's outcome. This can involve moral decisions, strategic choices, and interactions with NPCs. Ensuring that player choices have tangible consequences enhances immersion and investment in the game.

The theory of world-building is also integral to RPG design. Creating a believable and immersive game world involves careful attention to detail, including the game's lore, geography, cultures, and history. A well-crafted world can draw players in and make their adventures feel more meaningful. This involves not only visual and auditory design but also the creation of consistent rules and logic that govern the game world.

Gameplay mechanics in RPGs are designed to support the narrative and character development. This includes combat systems, magic and abilities, inventory management, and quest design. The theory of balanced mechanics ensures that different gameplay elements work together harmoniously, providing a challenging yet rewarding experience. Balancing mechanics also involves catering to different playstyles, such as combat-focused, stealth-oriented, or diplomatic approaches.

The concept of immersion is a key theoretical approach to RPGs. Immersion refers to the player's sense of being part of the game world. High levels of immersion can be achieved through detailed graphics, realistic sound design, and engaging storytelling. Additionally, minimizing interruptions, such as loading screens or inconsistent mechanics, helps maintain immersion.

Another theoretical approach is the integration of social elements in RPGs. Multiplayer RPGs and MMORPGs emphasize social interaction, cooperation, and competition among players. Theories of social dynamics and community building are important in designing features that encourage positive player interactions and a sense of belonging within the game world.

Procedural content generation is a theoretical approach that involves using algorithms to create game content dynamically. This can include generating levels, quests, and even entire worlds. Procedural generation can enhance replayability and provide unique experiences for each player. However, it requires careful design to ensure that procedurally generated content remains coherent and engaging.

The theory of player motivation explores what drives players to engage with RPGs. This can include intrinsic motivations, such as the desire for exploration, storytelling, and character growth, as well as extrinsic motivations, such as rewards, achievements, and social recognition. Understanding player motivation helps designers create experiences that resonate with their audience.

Finally, the ethical considerations in RPG design are an important theoretical aspect. This involves addressing issues such as representation, inclusivity, and the impact of player choices. Ensuring that RPGs offer diverse and respectful portrayals of characters and cultures can enhance the game's appeal and create a more inclusive environment for players.

In conclusion, theoretical approaches to RPGs encompass a wide range of concepts, including narrative structure, character development, player agency, world-building, gameplay mechanics, immersion, social dynamics, procedural generation, player motivation, and ethical considerations. These theories provide a framework for understanding what makes RPGs engaging and immersive, guiding designers in creating compelling and memorable experiences for players.

Strategy Games: Planning and Execution Theories

Strategy games are a genre that emphasizes planning, decision-making, and resource management. The theoretical approaches to strategy games focus on the mechanics of planning and execution, which are crucial for creating engaging and challenging gameplay experiences. These theories explore how players formulate strategies, make decisions, and adapt to changing circumstances within the game.

One of the core theories in strategy game design is the concept of strategic planning. Strategic planning involves long-term goal setting and the formulation of a plan to achieve those goals. In strategy games, players must analyze their current situation, anticipate future challenges, and allocate resources effectively. This process requires critical thinking and foresight, as players must consider multiple variables and potential outcomes.

Resource management is another key theoretical approach in strategy games. Players are often tasked with managing limited resources, such as money, manpower, and materials. Effective resource management involves prioritizing expenditures, optimizing production, and making trade-offs. This adds a layer of complexity to the game, as players must balance immediate needs with long-term objectives.

The theory of decision-making is central to strategy games. Players are constantly faced with choices that can significantly impact their progress. These decisions can range from tactical maneuvers in combat to economic investments and diplomatic negotiations. Understanding the consequences of each decision and weighing the risks and rewards is a critical skill in strategy games.

Adaptability and flexibility are important theoretical concepts in strategy game design. Players must be able to adapt their strategies in response to changing circumstances, such as enemy actions, environmental factors, and random events. This requires a dynamic approach to planning, where players must continually reassess their situation and adjust their strategies accordingly.

The theory of game balance is crucial in ensuring that strategy games are challenging yet fair. Game balance involves creating systems and mechanics that provide a level playing field for all players. This includes balancing different factions, units, and abilities to ensure that no single strategy or approach is overwhelmingly dominant. Achieving balance requires careful testing and iteration to fine-tune the game's mechanics.

Complexity and depth are theoretical aspects that contribute to the richness of strategy games. Complexity refers to the number of variables and systems that players must consider, while depth refers to the strategic options and interactions available. A well-designed strategy game offers a balance between complexity and depth, providing enough challenge to engage players without overwhelming them.

The concept of fog of war is a common theoretical approach in strategy games. Fog of war limits the player's knowledge of the game map and enemy positions, adding an element of uncertainty and requiring reconnaissance and information gathering. This mechanic enhances the realism and challenge of the game, as players must make decisions based on incomplete information.

Turn-based and real-time mechanics are two distinct theoretical approaches in strategy games. Turn-based strategy (TBS) games, such as "Civilization," allow players to take their time to plan and execute their moves, providing a more deliberate and thoughtful gameplay experience. Real-time strategy (RTS) games, such as "StarCraft," require quick thinking and rapid decision-making, creating a more intense and fast-paced experience. Each approach offers unique challenges and appeals to different player preferences.

The integration of multiplayer elements is another important theoretical aspect of strategy games. Multiplayer strategy games allow players to compete against or cooperate with others, adding a social dimension to the gameplay. Theories of player interaction and competition are crucial in designing features that support balanced and engaging multiplayer experiences.

Finally, the theory of emergent gameplay explores how complex behaviors and strategies can arise from simple rules and mechanics. Emergent gameplay occurs when players discover innovative ways to interact with the game systems, creating unique and unexpected outcomes. This adds a layer of depth and replayability to strategy games, as players can continually explore new strategies and approaches.

In conclusion, the theoretical approaches to strategy games encompass a wide range of concepts, including strategic planning, resource management, decision-making, adaptability, game balance, complexity and depth, fog of war, turn-based and real-time mechanics, multiplayer elements, and emergent gameplay. These theories provide a framework for understanding what makes strategy games engaging and challenging, guiding designers in creating compelling and memorable experiences for players.

Sports and Simulation Games: Realism and Abstraction

Sports and simulation games aim to replicate real-world activities and experiences, often striving for a balance between realism and abstraction. The theoretical approaches to these genres explore how developers create engaging gameplay that accurately represents real-life elements while remaining accessible and enjoyable for players.

One of the primary theories in sports and simulation game design is the concept of realism. Realism involves accurately modeling the physical and mechanical aspects of the real-world activity being simulated. In sports games, this can include realistic player movements, accurate physics, and authentic game rules. For example, the "FIFA" series strives to replicate the intricacies of soccer, from player behavior to ball dynamics. Realism enhances immersion and provides players with an experience that closely mirrors the real world.

Abstraction is another crucial theoretical approach, involving the simplification and generalization of real-world elements to create a more manageable and enjoyable gameplay experience. While realism focuses on accuracy, abstraction emphasizes playability. For example, a racing simulation like "Forza Motorsport" may simplify certain aspects of car mechanics to make the game more accessible to casual players. Striking a balance between realism and abstraction is essential to ensure that the game is both engaging and approachable.

The theory of control and input mechanisms is central to sports and simulation games. These games often require precise and intuitive controls to replicate the real-world activity accurately. In sports games, players need to perform complex actions with ease, such as dribbling, passing, and shooting in basketball. Simulation games, like flight simulators, require detailed control schemes to manage various aspects of the simulated experience. Designing controls that are both realistic and user-friendly is a key challenge.

The concept of player agency is important in these genres, referring to the degree of control and influence players have over the game's events and outcomes. High player agency allows for meaningful decisions and actions that directly impact the game. In sports games, this can involve strategic choices, such as team management and playcalling. In simulation games, player agency can include building and managing cities in "SimCity" or controlling an entire civilization in "Civilization." Ensuring that players have a significant impact on the game enhances engagement and satisfaction.

The theory of progression and achievement is relevant to sports and simulation games. Players are motivated by a sense of growth and accomplishment, which can be achieved through various progression systems. In sports games, this can involve improving player skills, winning championships, and unlocking new content. In simulation games, progression can be achieved through expanding and improving the simulated environment, such as growing a city or developing new technologies. Providing clear goals and rewards helps maintain player interest and motivation.

Multiplayer elements are a significant theoretical aspect of sports and simulation games. Competing against or cooperating with other players adds a social dimension to the gameplay. In sports games, multiplayer modes allow players to compete in matches and tournaments, while simulation games can include cooperative city-building or competitive strategy elements. Designing balanced and engaging multiplayer experiences requires careful consideration of player interaction and competition.

The theory of adaptability and dynamic systems is crucial in simulation games. These games often involve complex systems that change and evolve based on player actions and external factors. For example, in a city-building game, the economy, population, and environment can all be affected by player decisions and random events. Ensuring that these systems are dynamic and responsive adds depth and realism to the game, providing a more engaging experience.

Educational aspects are also a theoretical consideration in simulation games. Many simulation games are designed to teach players about real-world processes and systems. For example, flight simulators can provide valuable training for aspiring pilots, while business simulations can teach management and economic principles. Balancing educational content with engaging gameplay is essential to create effective and enjoyable educational simulations.

The integration of narrative elements is a theoretical approach that can enhance sports and simulation games. While these genres are often focused on gameplay mechanics, incorporating a compelling narrative can add depth and context. In sports games, a career mode with a storyline can provide motivation and emotional investment. In simulation games, narratives can emerge from the player's actions and decisions, creating a more immersive experience.

In conclusion, the theoretical approaches to sports and simulation games involve a balance between realism and abstraction, control and input mechanisms, player agency, progression and achievement, multiplayer elements, adaptability and dynamic systems, educational aspects, and narrative integration. These theories provide a framework for understanding what makes these genres engaging and immersive, guiding designers in creating compelling and realistic experiences for players.

Puzzles and Casual Games: Cognitive Theories

Puzzle and casual games are designed to be accessible, engaging, and mentally stimulating. The theoretical approaches to these genres often focus on cognitive theories, exploring how players solve problems, learn, and engage with the game. Understanding these theories can help designers create games that are both challenging and enjoyable.

One of the primary cognitive theories in puzzle game design is the concept of problem-solving. Puzzle games challenge players to think critically and use logic to solve various problems. This can involve recognizing patterns, manipulating objects, and finding solutions to complex challenges. Games like "Tetris" and "The Witness" exemplify this approach, requiring players to use their cognitive skills to progress.

The theory of learning and progression is crucial in puzzle and casual games. These games often introduce new mechanics and challenges gradually, allowing players to learn and master them over time. This approach helps maintain player engagement and prevents frustration. For example, in a game like "Portal," players start with simple puzzles that gradually become more complex as they learn to use the game's mechanics effectively.

Cognitive load theory is another important consideration in puzzle and casual game design. This theory suggests that games should balance the difficulty of challenges to avoid overwhelming players. A well-designed game manages cognitive load by providing clear instructions, visual cues, and incremental difficulty. This ensures that players remain engaged without becoming frustrated or bored.

The concept of flow is central to puzzle and casual games. Flow refers to a state of deep focus and immersion where players lose track of time and are fully engaged in the game. Achieving flow involves creating a balance between challenge and skill, ensuring that players are constantly engaged without feeling overwhelmed or under-challenged. Games like "Candy Crush" and "Bejeweled" are designed to create a flow state by offering a series of progressively challenging puzzles.

The theory of intrinsic and extrinsic motivation is relevant to puzzle and casual games. Intrinsic motivation comes from the enjoyment of the game itself, while extrinsic motivation comes from external rewards, such as points, achievements, and progression. Successful puzzle and casual games often combine both types of motivation, providing satisfying gameplay while also rewarding players for their accomplishments.

Pattern recognition is a cognitive process that is heavily utilized in puzzle games. Players must identify and interpret patterns to solve puzzles and progress. This can involve visual patterns, numerical sequences, or logical relationships. Games like "Sudoku" and "Picross" rely on players' ability to recognize and manipulate patterns to achieve their goals.

Memory and recall are also important cognitive processes in puzzle and casual games. Some games challenge players to remember sequences, locations, or details to solve puzzles. For example, in "Memory" or "Match-3" games, players must remember the positions of tiles or items to make successful matches. These games help improve memory and recall skills while providing engaging gameplay.

The theory of user interface (UI) design is crucial in casual games. These games often have simple and intuitive interfaces that allow players to understand and interact with the game easily. Clear visual and auditory feedback, intuitive controls, and minimalistic design help create a seamless and enjoyable experience. Games like "Angry Birds" and "Cut the Rope" are known for their user-friendly interfaces that enhance the overall gameplay experience.

The social and community aspects of casual games are also important theoretical considerations. Many casual games incorporate social features, such as leaderboards, multiplayer modes, and social sharing options. These features encourage players to engage with friends and the broader community, adding a social dimension to the gameplay. Social interaction and competition can enhance motivation and retention in casual games.

Accessibility is a key theoretical aspect of puzzle and casual games. These games are designed to be easy to pick up and play, making them accessible to a wide audience, including those who may not consider themselves gamers. Simple mechanics, short play sessions, and intuitive design help make these games approachable and enjoyable for players of all ages and skill levels.

In conclusion, the theoretical approaches to puzzle and casual games involve cognitive theories of problem-solving, learning and progression, cognitive load, flow, intrinsic and extrinsic motivation, pattern recognition, memory and recall, user interface design, social and community aspects, and accessibility. These theories provide a framework for understanding what makes these genres engaging and mentally stimulating, guiding designers in creating games that are both challenging and enjoyable for a wide audience.

Chapter 6: Player Interaction and Social Gaming

The Theory of Player Interaction

Player interaction is a fundamental aspect of game design, encompassing the ways in which players engage with the game and each other. The theoretical approaches to player interaction explore the dynamics of these interactions and how they can be designed to enhance the gaming experience.

One of the core theories in player interaction is the concept of social presence. Social presence refers to the sense of being with other players in a virtual environment. High social presence can enhance immersion and engagement, making players feel more connected to the game and each other. This can be achieved through features such as in-game chat, voice communication, and avatars that represent players in the game world.

The theory of cooperation and competition is central to multiplayer game design. Cooperative gameplay involves players working together to achieve common goals, fostering teamwork and camaraderie. Competitive gameplay, on the other hand, pits players against each other, creating a sense of rivalry and challenge. Balancing cooperation and competition is crucial to create engaging multiplayer experiences that cater to different player preferences.

The concept of player agency is important in player interaction. High player agency allows players to make meaningful choices that impact the game and their interactions with others. This can include decisions about how to approach challenges, interact with NPCs, and collaborate or compete with other players. Ensuring that player choices have tangible consequences enhances engagement and investment in the game.

The theory of emergent gameplay explores how player interactions can lead to unexpected and unique experiences. Emergent gameplay occurs when players use the game's mechanics and systems in creative ways, often leading to new strategies and social dynamics. Encouraging emergent gameplay requires flexible and open-ended game design that allows for player creativity and experimentation.

Social dynamics and community building are crucial theoretical aspects of player interaction. Successful multiplayer games often foster strong communities where players can connect, share experiences, and support each other. Features such as guilds, clans, and leaderboards can help build a sense of belonging and identity within the game. Community management is also important to ensure a positive and inclusive environment for all players.

The theory of user-generated content involves allowing players to create and share their own content within the game. This can include custom levels, mods, and in-game items. User-generated content can enhance player engagement and extend the lifespan of the game by providing a constant stream of new and diverse content. It also empowers players to contribute to the game's development and share their creativity with others.

The concept of matchmaking and player balance is important in competitive multiplayer games. Effective matchmaking systems ensure that players are matched with others of similar skill levels, creating fair and challenging gameplay. Player balance involves designing game mechanics and systems that prevent any single strategy or playstyle from dominating, ensuring a diverse and dynamic competitive environment.

The theory of player motivation explores what drives players to engage with multiplayer games. This can include intrinsic motivations, such as the enjoyment of gameplay and social interaction, as well as extrinsic motivations, such as rewards, achievements, and recognition. Understanding player motivation helps designers create experiences that resonate with their audience and keep them coming back.

The concept of toxicity and player behavior is an important theoretical aspect of player interaction. Toxic behavior, such as harassment and cheating, can significantly impact the gaming experience and community health. Designing systems to mitigate toxic behavior, such as reporting mechanisms, moderation tools, and positive reinforcement, is crucial to maintaining a positive and inclusive gaming environment.

Finally, the integration of cross-platform play is a growing trend in multiplayer game design. Cross-platform play allows players on different devices to compete and cooperate in the same game, breaking down barriers between platforms. This enhances the player base and creates a more inclusive and diverse gaming community. Designing for cross-platform play involves technical and design challenges, such as ensuring compatibility and balancing controls across different devices.

In conclusion, the theoretical approaches to player interaction encompass social presence, cooperation and competition, player agency, emergent gameplay, social dynamics, user-generated content, matchmaking and player balance, player motivation, toxicity and player behavior, and cross-platform play. These theories provide a framework for understanding what makes multiplayer games engaging and how to design interactions that enhance the gaming experience. By leveraging these theories, designers can create compelling and dynamic multiplayer games that foster strong communities and provide memorable experiences for players.

Chapter 7: Player Interaction and Social Gaming

The Theory of Player Interaction

Player interaction is a fundamental aspect of game design that shapes the overall gaming experience. Interaction can be broadly classified into two types: player-to-player and player-to-environment. Understanding these interactions is crucial for creating engaging and immersive games.

Player-to-player interaction encompasses all forms of direct and indirect communication between players. This includes competitive elements such as PvP (Player vs. Player) combat, cooperative gameplay, trading, and socializing. Effective design of player-to-player interactions can enhance the social experience and encourage community building within the game.

Player-to-environment interaction refers to the ways players engage with the game world and its mechanics. This includes exploring environments, solving puzzles, interacting with NPCs (non-player characters), and manipulating game objects. Designing intuitive and rewarding player-to-environment interactions is essential for maintaining player engagement.

Balancing these interactions requires a deep understanding of player psychology and behavior. Game designers must anticipate how players will interact with each other and the game world, and design systems that facilitate enjoyable and meaningful interactions.

The Impact of Game Mechanics on Interaction

Game mechanics play a pivotal role in shaping player interactions. Mechanics such as chat systems, emotes, and guilds facilitate social interaction, while mechanics like quests, challenges, and leaderboards drive competitive and cooperative gameplay. The design of these mechanics should consider the desired social dynamics and the overall game experience.

For example, in massively multiplayer online games (MMOs), mechanics like guilds and alliances promote long-term social bonds and cooperative gameplay. In contrast, competitive games like MOBAs (Multiplayer Online Battle Arenas) emphasize mechanics that foster rivalry and team strategy.

Social Interaction and Player Retention

Strong social interaction is a key factor in player retention. Games that provide opportunities for players to form friendships and social networks often see higher retention rates. Social features such as friend lists, chat rooms, and in-game events encourage players to return to the game regularly.

Designers can leverage social psychology principles, such as social proof and reciprocity, to enhance player interaction. For instance, rewarding players for helping others can foster a sense of community and encourage positive interactions.

Case Studies: Successful Social Games

Analyzing successful social games can provide valuable insights into effective player interaction design. Games like "World of Warcraft," "Fortnite," and "Among Us" have built strong player communities through well-designed social features and mechanics.

"World of Warcraft" excels in creating long-term social bonds through guilds, raids, and social events. "Fortnite" uses dynamic social interactions, such as in-game concerts and events, to keep the community engaged. "Among Us" capitalizes on social deduction mechanics to create intense and memorable player interactions.

Designing for Multiplayer Experiences

Designing for multiplayer experiences involves creating systems that facilitate seamless and enjoyable interactions between players. This requires a deep understanding of network architecture, matchmaking algorithms, and user interface design.

Matchmaking and Balancing

Effective matchmaking is crucial for creating balanced and fair multiplayer experiences. Matchmaking algorithms should consider factors such as player skill level, latency, and game mode preferences. Balancing these factors ensures that players are matched with appropriate opponents or teammates, enhancing the overall gameplay experience.

Network Architecture

The network architecture of a game significantly impacts the quality of multiplayer experiences. Reliable and low-latency connections are essential for real-time interactions. Designers must consider server infrastructure, data synchronization, and error handling to provide a smooth and responsive multiplayer experience.

User Interface Design for Multiplayer

User interface (UI) design plays a critical role in facilitating multiplayer interactions. The UI should provide clear and intuitive controls for communication, team coordination, and gameplay actions. Elements like chat windows, minimaps, and status indicators help players stay informed and engaged.

Case Studies: Multiplayer Game Design

Examining successful multiplayer games can offer insights into effective design practices. Games like "League of Legends," "Overwatch," and "Minecraft" have mastered the art of multiplayer experience design through innovative matchmaking, robust network infrastructure, and user-friendly interfaces.

"League of Legends" uses a sophisticated matchmaking system that considers multiple factors to create balanced matches. "Overwatch" emphasizes team coordination through clear and intuitive UI elements. "Minecraft" provides an open-ended multiplayer experience that encourages creativity and collaboration.

Social Dynamics in Games

Social dynamics in games refer to the patterns of interaction and behavior that emerge within player communities. Understanding these dynamics is essential for designing games that foster positive and engaging social experiences.

Emergent Behavior

Emergent behavior occurs when players interact in ways that are not explicitly designed by the game developers. This can lead to the creation of unique social norms, cultures, and gameplay strategies. Designers should anticipate and support emergent behavior to enhance the depth and richness of the game world.

Toxicity and Community Management

Managing toxicity is a significant challenge in multiplayer games. Toxic behavior, such as harassment and griefing, can negatively impact the player experience and community health. Effective community management strategies, such as moderation, reporting systems, and positive reinforcement, are crucial for maintaining a healthy player environment.

Fostering Positive Social Dynamics

Designers can foster positive social dynamics by encouraging cooperation, empathy, and sportsmanship. Features such as collaborative missions, team-based rewards, and player recognition systems can promote positive interactions and a supportive community.

Case Studies: Social Dynamics

Analyzing the social dynamics of successful games can provide valuable insights into effective community management. Games like "Animal Crossing: New Horizons," "Apex Legends," and "Guild Wars 2" have created positive and engaging player communities through thoughtful design and management practices.

"Animal Crossing: New Horizons" fosters a friendly and cooperative community through its laid-back gameplay and social features. "Apex Legends" encourages teamwork and sportsmanship through its ping system and team-based rewards. "Guild Wars 2" promotes a supportive player community through collaborative world events and dynamic group content.

Community Management and Player Retention

Community management involves actively engaging with the player base to foster a positive and supportive environment. Effective community management can significantly impact player retention and satisfaction.

The Role of Community Managers

Community managers act as the bridge between the players and the developers. They facilitate communication, gather feedback, and address player concerns. Their role is crucial in building trust and maintaining a healthy player community.

Player Feedback and Iteration

Gathering and responding to player feedback is essential for continuous improvement. Community managers should actively listen to player concerns, identify common issues, and communicate these to the development team. Regular updates and transparent communication can help build player trust and loyalty.

Case Studies: Effective Community Management

Successful games often have robust community management practices. Games like "Destiny 2," "Final Fantasy XIV," and "Rainbow Six Siege" have built strong player communities through effective engagement and communication.

"Destiny 2" excels in transparent communication through regular developer updates and community interactions. "Final Fantasy XIV" maintains a supportive community through active moderation and player recognition.

"Rainbow Six Siege" continuously improves the game based on player feedback and community input.

Case Studies: Successful Community Building

Case studies of successful community building can provide valuable lessons for game designers. Examining the strategies and practices of games that have built strong player communities can offer insights into effective community management.

"World of Warcraft"

"World of Warcraft" is a prime example of successful community building. The game has maintained a strong player base for over a decade through its guild system, social events, and continuous content updates. The game's community-driven content, such as raids and player-created events, has fostered a deep sense of camaraderie and belonging among players.

"Fortnite"

"Fortnite" has built a massive player community through its dynamic events and social features. The game's in-game events, such as concerts and live events, create shared experiences that bring players together. The continuous addition of new content and collaboration with popular franchises keeps the community engaged and excited.

"Among Us"

"Among Us" became a cultural phenomenon through its social deduction gameplay and community-driven content. The game's simplicity and accessibility allowed players to create their own social experiences, leading to a massive and engaged player base. Community-created mods and content have further enhanced the game's social dynamics.

Chapter 8: Level Design and World Building

Principles of Level Design

Level design is the process of creating the environments and stages in which players interact. Effective level design balances aesthetics, gameplay mechanics, and narrative elements to create engaging and immersive experiences.

The Role of Space and Layout

The spatial layout of a level significantly impacts the player experience. Designers must consider the flow of movement, the placement of obstacles, and the arrangement of interactive elements. A well-designed layout guides players intuitively, encouraging exploration and interaction.

Balancing Challenge and Reward

Balancing challenge and reward is crucial in level design. Levels should provide a gradual increase in difficulty, allowing players to develop their skills and feel a sense of accomplishment. Rewards, such as collectibles, power-ups, and narrative revelations, should be strategically placed to motivate and satisfy players.

Visual and Thematic Cohesion

Visual and thematic cohesion enhances the immersion and narrative impact of a level. Consistent use of visual elements, color schemes, and thematic motifs helps create a believable and engaging game world. Designers should align the visual design with the narrative and gameplay objectives of the level.

Case Studies: Iconic Level Designs

Analyzing iconic level designs can provide valuable insights into effective level design principles. Games like "Super Mario Bros.," "The Legend of Zelda: Breath of the Wild," and "Dark Souls" have created memorable and impactful levels through thoughtful design.

"Super Mario Bros." excels in teaching players new mechanics through level design. "The Legend of Zelda: Breath of the Wild" offers an open-world design that encourages exploration and discovery. "Dark Souls" uses interconnected levels to create a sense of a cohesive and challenging world.

Creating Immersive Game Worlds

Creating immersive game worlds involves designing environments that feel believable and engaging. Immersion is achieved through a combination of visual design, interactive elements, and narrative integration.

Environmental Storytelling

Environmental storytelling uses the design of the game world to convey narrative elements. Details such as props, architecture, and environmental cues can provide context and backstory without explicit exposition. This technique enhances immersion and encourages players to explore and discover the narrative organically.

Interactive Environments

Interactive environments engage players by allowing them to manipulate and interact with the game world. Elements such as destructible objects, dynamic weather, and interactive NPCs create a sense of a living and responsive world. Designers should consider how these interactions contribute to the overall gameplay experience.

Sound and Music in World Building

Sound and music play a crucial role in creating an immersive game world. Ambient sounds, music, and audio cues enhance the atmosphere and emotional impact of the environment. Designers should use audio elements to complement the visual design and reinforce the narrative themes.

Case Studies: Immersive Game Worlds

Examining immersive game worlds can provide insights into effective world-building techniques. Games like "The Elder Scrolls V: Skyrim," "Red Dead Redemption 2," and "Bioshock" have created rich and engaging worlds through detailed design and narrative integration.

"The Elder Scrolls V: Skyrim" offers a vast and diverse world filled with interactive elements and lore. "Red Dead Redemption 2" creates a realistic and immersive world through meticulous attention to detail and dynamic interactions. "Bioshock" uses environmental storytelling and audio design to create a haunting and immersive atmosphere.

Spatial Theories and Player Navigation

Spatial theories in level design focus on how players perceive and navigate game environments. Understanding these theories helps designers create levels that are intuitive, engaging, and enjoyable to explore.

The Concept of Spatial Awareness

Spatial awareness refers to the player's ability to understand and navigate the game environment. Designers can enhance spatial awareness through clear visual cues, intuitive layout, and consistent design elements. Techniques such as landmarks, pathways, and sightlines help guide players through the level.

The Role of Cognitive Mapping

Cognitive mapping involves the mental representation of the game environment. Players create cognitive maps to navigate and remember important locations and routes. Designers can support cognitive mapping by creating distinct and memorable areas, providing maps and markers, and using consistent visual language.

Flow and Pacing in Level Design

Flow and pacing are crucial for maintaining player engagement. Levels should provide a balance of challenge and rest, guiding players through a sequence of engaging and varied experiences. Designers should consider the pacing of encounters, puzzles, and narrative elements to create a smooth and enjoyable flow.

Case Studies: Spatial Theories in Practice

Analyzing games that effectively use spatial theories can provide valuable insights for level design. Games like "Portal," "Half-Life 2," and "Uncharted 4" excel in guiding players through complex environments and maintaining a strong sense of flow and pacing.

"Portal" uses visual and spatial cues to guide players through puzzle-based levels. "Half-Life 2" combines linear and open environments to create a dynamic and engaging experience. "Uncharted 4" uses landmarks, pathways, and visual storytelling to create a seamless and immersive adventure.

Environmental Storytelling

Environmental storytelling uses the design of the game world to convey narrative elements. This technique enhances immersion and encourages players to explore and discover the narrative organically.

The Role of Props and Details

Props and details within the environment provide context and backstory. Items such as notes, graffiti, and environmental damage can convey information about the game's world and its inhabitants. Designers should use these elements to create a rich and believable environment.

Architecture and Design Language

The architecture and design language of the game world contribute to environmental storytelling. The style, structure, and layout of buildings and environments can reflect the culture, history, and narrative themes of the game. Consistent and thoughtful design language enhances the immersion and believability of the world.

Interactive Story Elements

Interactive story elements, such as NPCs and dynamic events, engage players and reinforce the narrative. Designers should consider how these elements contribute to the overall story and player experience. Interactive elements should feel natural and integrated into the game world.

Case Studies: Environmental Storytelling

Examining games that excel in environmental storytelling can provide insights into effective techniques. Games like "The Last of Us," "Bloodborne," and "Dishonored" use environmental storytelling to create rich and immersive narratives.

"The Last of Us" uses props and environmental details to convey the story of a post-apocalyptic world. "Bloodborne" uses architecture and design language to create a haunting and atmospheric environment. "Dishonored" combines interactive story elements with environmental cues to create a dynamic and engaging narrative.

Challenges in Modern Level Design

Modern level design faces several challenges, including increased player expectations, technological advancements, and the need for innovation. Designers must navigate these challenges to create engaging and memorable levels.

Balancing Innovation and Familiarity

Balancing innovation and familiarity is crucial in level design. Players appreciate new and unique experiences but also value familiar mechanics and design elements. Designers should strive to innovate within established frameworks to create engaging and accessible levels.

Adapting to Technological Advancements

Technological advancements offer new opportunities and challenges for level design. Improved graphics, physics, and AI can enhance the player experience but also require more complex and resource-intensive design processes. Designers must stay informed about new technologies and adapt their workflows accordingly.

Meeting Player Expectations

Player expectations have increased with the growth of the gaming industry. Modern players expect high-quality graphics, seamless performance, and engaging gameplay. Designers must prioritize player experience and continually iterate on their designs to meet these expectations.

Case Studies: Overcoming Level Design Challenges

Analyzing games that have successfully overcome level design challenges can provide valuable lessons. Games like "The Witcher 3: Wild Hunt," "God of War," and "Cyberpunk 2077" have navigated the complexities of modern level design to create impactful and memorable experiences.

"The Witcher 3: Wild Hunt" balances innovation and familiarity through its open-world design and engaging quests. "God of War" adapts to technological advancements with stunning graphics and seamless gameplay. "Cyberpunk 2077" meets player expectations through its ambitious world-building and narrative depth.

UI/UX Challenges in Modern Games

UI/UX design in modern games involves creating intuitive and enjoyable interfaces that enhance the player experience. Designers face several challenges, including complexity, accessibility, and consistency.

Balancing Complexity and Simplicity

Balancing complexity and simplicity is crucial in UI/UX design. Interfaces should provide all necessary information and controls without overwhelming the player. Designers should prioritize clarity and usability, using techniques such as visual hierarchy and intuitive navigation.

Ensuring Accessibility

Accessibility is a key consideration in modern game design. Interfaces should be usable by players with diverse abilities and preferences. Designers can incorporate features such as customizable controls, screen readers, and colorblind modes to enhance accessibility.

Maintaining Consistency

Consistency in UI/UX design helps create a cohesive and intuitive player experience. Designers should use consistent visual elements, terminology, and interaction patterns throughout the game. Consistency enhances usability and reduces player frustration.

Case Studies: UI/UX Innovations

Examining games that excel in UI/UX design can provide valuable insights. Games like "Horizon Zero Dawn," "Celeste," and "The Division 2" have created intuitive and engaging interfaces through innovative design practices.

"Horizon Zero Dawn" balances complexity and simplicity with its clear and intuitive HUD. "Celeste" ensures accessibility through customizable controls and assist modes. "The Division 2" maintains consistency with its cohesive and user-friendly interface design.

Building a Successful Game Development Culture

Creating a positive and productive game development culture involves fostering collaboration, innovation, and well-being within the team. A successful culture can enhance creativity, reduce burnout, and improve the overall quality of the game.

Promoting Collaboration and Communication

Collaboration and communication are essential for a successful game development culture. Teams should use tools and practices that facilitate clear and open communication, such as regular meetings, collaborative software, and transparent workflows.

Encouraging Innovation

Encouraging innovation involves creating an environment where team members feel empowered to experiment and take risks. This can be achieved through flexible workflows, support for creative initiatives, and recognition of innovative contributions.

Prioritizing Well-being

Prioritizing well-being is crucial for maintaining a healthy and productive team. Developers should have access to resources and support for managing stress, maintaining work-life balance, and promoting mental health. Creating a supportive and inclusive workplace culture can enhance overall well-being and job satisfaction.

Case Studies: Successful Game Development Cultures

Analyzing studios with successful game development cultures can provide valuable insights. Studios like Naughty Dog, Bungie, and Supergiant Games have created positive and productive environments through thoughtful cultural practices.

Naughty Dog promotes collaboration and communication through its open and inclusive studio culture. Bungie encourages innovation by supporting creative initiatives and experimental projects. Supergiant Games prioritizes well-being through flexible work schedules and a supportive team environment.

Chapter 9: The Narrative Paradigm

Storytelling in Games

Storytelling in games has evolved significantly over the years, moving from simple text-based adventures to complex, interactive narratives that rival the depth of novels and films. The narrative structure in games is not just an added layer but an integral part of the gaming experience. It provides context, motivation, and emotional depth, enhancing the player's engagement and immersion.

A compelling story can make or break a game. It's the difference between a forgettable experience and one that players remember and discuss for years. The unique aspect of storytelling in games is its interactivity. Unlike traditional media, games allow players to influence the story, making each experience personal and unique.

Interactive storytelling requires careful balancing. Developers must ensure that the player's choices have meaningful consequences, while still guiding them through a coherent and engaging plot. This balance is often achieved through branching narratives, where different choices lead to different outcomes, creating a web of possibilities.

Branching narratives, however, come with their own challenges. They require extensive planning and writing to ensure that all possible story paths are well-developed and satisfying. This complexity can lead to increased development time and costs, but the payoff in player engagement can be substantial.

One effective technique in game storytelling is environmental storytelling. This involves using the game world itself to convey narrative elements. Objects, architecture, and even lighting can provide clues about the story, encouraging players to explore and piece together the narrative on their own. This method not only enriches the story but also deepens the player's connection to the game world.

Dialogue and character development are also crucial components of game storytelling. Well-written characters with distinct personalities, backgrounds, and motivations can make the story more relatable and engaging. Voice acting and motion capture technology have further enhanced character realism, allowing for more nuanced and emotional performances.

Another important aspect is pacing. Unlike films or books, games can vary greatly in length, and players may progress at different rates. Developers must ensure that the story maintains its momentum, providing regular narrative beats to keep players engaged. This can be achieved through main story missions, side quests, and in-game events.

Games also offer unique opportunities for non-linear storytelling. Open-world games, for example, allow players to tackle missions and objectives in any order, creating a more personalized narrative experience. This non-linearity can enhance replayability, as players may discover new story elements and outcomes in subsequent playthroughs.

In conclusion, storytelling in games is a dynamic and multifaceted process. It combines traditional narrative techniques with interactive elements to create immersive and engaging experiences. As technology and game design continue to evolve, so too will the possibilities for storytelling in games, offering ever more complex and captivating narratives for players to explore.

Narrative Structures and Archetypes

Narrative structures and archetypes play a crucial role in shaping the stories in games. These elements provide a framework that guides the development of the plot and characters, ensuring that the story resonates with players on a deeper level. Understanding and effectively utilizing these structures and archetypes can significantly enhance the storytelling in games.

One of the most common narrative structures in games is the Hero's Journey, a monomyth identified by Joseph Campbell. This structure involves a hero who embarks on an adventure, faces and overcomes a crisis, and then returns transformed. This journey is divided into stages, such as the Call to Adventure, the Road of Trials, and the Return. The Hero's Journey is prevalent in many games, from classic RPGs to modern action-adventures, due to its universal appeal and flexibility.

Another widely used structure is the Three-Act Structure, which divides the story into three parts: Setup, Confrontation, and Resolution. In the first act, the setting, characters, and conflict are introduced. The second act involves the protagonist facing various challenges and escalating conflicts. The third act resolves the story, often with a climax and a resolution. This structure is effective in maintaining a clear and engaging narrative flow.

Archetypes are recurring character types or symbols that are universally recognized and resonate with players. Common archetypes in games include the Hero, the Mentor, the Shadow (villain), and the Trickster. These archetypes help in creating relatable and memorable characters. For example, the Mentor archetype, such as Gandalf in "The Lord of the Rings," provides guidance and wisdom to the hero, often aiding in their development.

Games also explore subversions and variations of traditional archetypes and structures to create unique and unexpected narratives. For instance, a game might feature an anti-hero instead of a traditional hero, or the narrative might unfold in a non-linear fashion, with players discovering the story through exploration and piecing together clues.

In addition to these classic structures and archetypes, games often incorporate branching narratives and multiple endings. This allows for a more personalized storytelling experience, where the player's choices directly impact the story's outcome. These branching paths can lead to different character arcs, plot twists, and resolutions, enhancing replayability and player investment.

Interactive storytelling also benefits from the use of environmental storytelling, where the game's world and setting convey narrative elements. This can include visual cues, hidden messages, and contextual details that enrich the story. For example, a desolate, abandoned city can tell a story of a past apocalypse, with remnants of the previous civilization scattered throughout the environment.

Moreover, games can blend different narrative structures and archetypes to create complex and layered stories. For example, a game might start with a linear narrative structure but gradually introduce branching paths and multiple endings as the player progresses. This hybrid approach can offer both a coherent main storyline and the freedom for players to shape their own experiences.

In summary, narrative structures and archetypes provide essential tools for game developers to craft engaging and immersive stories. By understanding and leveraging these elements, developers can create narratives that resonate with players, offering both familiarity and innovation. As the medium of gaming continues to evolve, so too will the ways in which stories are told, pushing the boundaries of interactive storytelling.

Interactive Narratives and Player Choice

Interactive narratives and player choice are fundamental aspects of modern game design, transforming the way stories are told and experienced. Unlike traditional media, games offer players the ability to influence the narrative, creating a more engaging and personalized experience. This interactivity is achieved through branching storylines, moral choices, and dynamic character interactions.

One of the primary methods of implementing interactive narratives is through branching storylines. These are narratives that split into multiple paths based on the player's decisions. Each choice can lead to different outcomes, affecting the story, characters, and even the game's world. This approach allows players to feel a sense of agency, as their actions have direct and meaningful consequences.

Moral choices are a common feature in interactive narratives, where players must make decisions that reflect their values and ethics. These choices often present dilemmas with no clear right or wrong answer, adding depth and complexity to the narrative. The impact of these decisions can range from altering character relationships to changing the entire course of the story. Games like "The Witcher" series and "Mass Effect" are renowned for their intricate moral choice systems.

Dynamic character interactions further enhance interactivity by allowing players to build relationships with in-game characters. These interactions can be influenced by the player's actions and dialogue choices, leading to different character arcs and story outcomes. For instance, befriending or antagonizing a particular character can unlock unique missions, dialogue, and endings.

Interactive narratives also benefit from non-linear storytelling, where players can explore the story at their own pace and in their preferred order. Open-world games like "The Elder Scrolls V: Skyrim" exemplify this approach, offering a vast, interconnected world with multiple questlines and story threads that players can pursue in any sequence.

To implement interactive narratives effectively, developers must consider the complexity and coherence of the branching paths. This often involves extensive planning and writing to ensure that all possible outcomes are well-developed and satisfying. Additionally, maintaining a balance between player agency and narrative direction is crucial. While players should feel that their choices matter, the overall story should still remain coherent and engaging.

The use of choice-and-consequence mechanics is another key element of interactive narratives. These mechanics track the player's decisions and apply consequences accordingly, creating a dynamic and responsive narrative. This can involve tracking reputation, morality, or relationship points, which influence how characters and the world react to the player.

Interactive narratives also open up opportunities for replayability. Players may want to experience different story paths and endings, encouraging multiple playthroughs. This not only extends the game's longevity but also deepens the player's connection to the story and characters.

Technological advancements have further enhanced the possibilities for interactive narratives. Sophisticated AI and machine learning can create more responsive and adaptive story systems, where the game dynamically adjusts the narrative based on player behavior. This can lead to more personalized and emergent storytelling experiences.

In conclusion, interactive narratives and player choice are transformative elements in game storytelling. They offer a level of engagement and personalization that traditional media cannot match, allowing players to shape their own stories and experiences. As technology and design techniques continue to evolve, the potential for interactive narratives will only expand, offering richer and more immersive storytelling opportunities.

Writing for Games: Challenges and Techniques

Writing for games presents unique challenges and requires distinct techniques compared to other forms of writing. The interactive nature of games demands a flexible and dynamic approach to storytelling, where the narrative must adapt to player actions and decisions. This section explores the key challenges and effective techniques for writing compelling game narratives.

One of the primary challenges in game writing is the need for non-linear storytelling. Unlike books or films, games often allow players to explore the story in any order. This non-linearity requires writers to create interconnected narrative threads that make sense regardless of the player's choices. Ensuring continuity and coherence across these threads is a complex task that demands meticulous planning and organization.

Another significant challenge is creating meaningful player choices. Players expect their decisions to have real consequences, which means writers must develop multiple story branches and outcomes. This involves writing extensive dialogue and narrative variations to account for different paths. Balancing these choices to ensure they are impactful without overwhelming the player is crucial.

Interactive dialogue is a key component of game writing. Players often engage in conversations with non-player characters (NPCs) that can influence the story and relationships. Writing dynamic and branching dialogue requires a deep understanding of character development and player psychology. Writers must anticipate player responses and provide options that are both logical and engaging.

Environmental storytelling is another essential technique in game writing. This involves using the game's world and environment to convey narrative elements. Objects, locations, and visual details can all contribute to the story, allowing players to piece together the narrative through exploration. This technique enhances immersion and encourages players to engage with the game world more deeply.

Balancing exposition and player agency is a delicate aspect of game writing. While it's important to provide enough context and background information, excessive exposition can hinder player immersion and agency. Writers must find creative ways to convey essential information without resorting to lengthy cutscenes or text dumps. This can be achieved through dialogue, environmental cues, and in-game events.

Character development is crucial in creating an engaging narrative. Players must feel a connection to the characters they interact with, which requires well-developed personalities, motivations, and arcs. Consistent and believable character behavior enhances immersion and emotional investment. Voice acting and motion capture can further bring characters to life, adding depth and nuance to their portrayal.

Pacing is another vital consideration in game writing. Unlike linear media, players may take varying amounts of time to progress through the story. Writers must ensure that the narrative maintains momentum and provides regular points of interest, regardless of the player's pace. This can be achieved through well-placed story beats, side quests, and in-game events.

Writing for different game genres also presents unique challenges. For example, role-playing games (RPGs) often require extensive world-building and character backstories, while action games may focus more on pacing and intense moments. Understanding the conventions and expectations of different genres is essential for effective game writing.

Collaboration is a key aspect of game writing. Writers often work closely with designers, artists, and programmers to integrate the narrative seamlessly into the gameplay. This collaborative process requires strong communication skills and a willingness to adapt and iterate on the story based on feedback and technical constraints.

In conclusion, writing for games is a multifaceted discipline that combines narrative creativity with technical precision. It involves addressing the unique challenges of interactivity, non-linearity, and player agency while employing techniques such as dynamic dialogue, environmental storytelling, and character development. As the medium of gaming continues to evolve, so too will the techniques and approaches to crafting compelling game narratives.

Case Studies: Games with Strong Narratives

Case studies of games with strong narratives provide valuable insights into the techniques and approaches that make these stories successful. Examining these examples helps to understand how different elements of game writing come together to create memorable and impactful experiences. This section highlights a few notable games renowned for their compelling narratives.

"The Last of Us" by Naughty Dog is often cited as a prime example of narrative excellence in gaming. The game combines a gripping story with well-developed characters and emotional depth. Set in a post-apocalyptic world, it follows the journey of Joel and Ellie as they navigate through dangerous environments and form a deep bond. The narrative is enriched by strong voice acting, motion capture, and meticulous attention to detail. The use of environmental storytelling and interactive dialogue further immerses players in the story.

"BioShock" by Irrational Games is another game known for its innovative narrative. Set in the underwater city of Rapture, the game explores themes of utopia, power, and morality. The story is revealed through audio diaries, environmental details, and character interactions, allowing players to piece together the narrative at their own pace. The twist ending, which challenges the player's perception of free will and control, is a testament to the game's storytelling prowess.

"The Witcher 3: Wild Hunt" by CD Projekt Red is celebrated for its expansive world and rich narrative. Based on the novels by Andrzej Sapkowski, the game follows Geralt of Rivia as he searches for his adopted daughter. The narrative is characterized by its branching paths and meaningful choices, allowing players to shape the story based on their decisions. The game features complex characters, moral dilemmas, and intricate subplots that enhance the main story.

"Red Dead Redemption 2" by Rockstar Games is praised for its immersive storytelling and character development. Set in the late 19th century, the game follows the decline of the Van der Linde gang through the eyes of Arthur Morgan. The narrative is deeply intertwined with the game's open world, with side missions and random encounters contributing to the overall story. The attention to historical detail and the emotional depth of the characters make the narrative compelling and engaging.

"Telltale's The Walking Dead" series is known for its episodic storytelling and player-driven narrative. Based on the comic book series by Robert Kirkman, the game focuses on the character of Clementine and her survival in a zombie apocalypse. The game's strength lies in its interactive dialogue and moral choices, which significantly impact the story's direction and outcome. The episodic format allows for cliffhangers and suspense, keeping players invested in the narrative.

"Life is Strange" by Dontnod Entertainment is another game that excels in narrative-driven gameplay. The game follows Max Caulfield, a high school student with the ability to rewind time. The story explores themes of friendship, loss, and identity, with player choices affecting the plot and character relationships. The episodic structure and strong character development create an emotional and immersive experience.

In conclusion, these case studies demonstrate the diverse approaches and techniques that contribute to strong game narratives. Whether through emotional character arcs, branching storylines, or immersive world-building, these games showcase the potential of interactive storytelling. By analyzing these examples, game developers can gain valuable insights into crafting compelling and memorable narratives in their own projects.

Chapter 10: Sound and Music in Games

The Role of Sound in Game Design

Sound plays a pivotal role in game design, significantly enhancing the player's experience and immersion. It encompasses everything from background music and sound effects to voice acting and ambient noises. Effective use of sound can evoke emotions, convey information, and create a more immersive and engaging game world.

Background music is one of the most recognizable elements of game sound design. It sets the tone and mood for different game scenes, whether it's the intense score during a boss battle or the serene melodies in a peaceful village. Music can also provide subtle cues about the game's world and story. For example, a shift in musical style can indicate a change in the game's environment or narrative.

Sound effects are another crucial component. They provide feedback for the player's actions, enhancing the sense of interaction and responsiveness. From the sound of footsteps to the clang of a sword, these effects make the game world feel more real and tangible. Well-designed sound effects can also provide important gameplay information, such as the direction of an enemy attack or the activation of a mechanism.

Voice acting brings characters to life, adding depth and personality to the game's narrative. Well-acted dialogue can make characters more relatable and engaging, helping players connect with the story. Voice acting also allows for more dynamic and expressive storytelling, with characters conveying emotions and nuances that text alone cannot achieve.

Ambient sounds and environmental audio contribute to the overall atmosphere of the game. These sounds, such as the rustling of leaves or the distant rumble of thunder, make the game world feel alive and immersive. They can also provide clues about the environment, such as the presence of nearby enemies or hidden secrets.

Interactive audio is a key aspect of sound design in games. Unlike linear media, games require audio that can respond to player actions in real-time. This includes dynamic music that changes based on the game's events, adaptive sound effects that vary with the environment, and voice lines that respond to player choices. This interactivity enhances the sense of immersion and makes the audio experience unique to each playthrough.

Implementing effective sound design requires collaboration between various disciplines, including composers, sound designers, programmers, and directors. This collaborative effort ensures that the audio elements align with the game's vision and gameplay mechanics. For example, the timing and intensity of music and sound effects must match the pacing and action of the game.

One of the challenges in game sound design is balancing audio elements to ensure clarity and cohesion. With multiple layers of sound, including music, effects, and dialogue, it's essential to mix them in a way that maintains their distinctiveness while creating a harmonious overall soundscape. This often involves techniques such as audio ducking, where the volume of one sound is lowered to make another more prominent.

Another important consideration is the technical aspect of sound implementation. Game audio must be optimized for various hardware and software configurations, ensuring consistent quality across different platforms. This includes considerations for sound compression, spatial audio, and performance optimization.

In conclusion, sound is a vital element of game design that significantly enhances the player's experience. It creates atmosphere, provides feedback, and brings the game world to life. Effective sound design requires a blend of artistic creativity and technical expertise, ensuring that audio elements work seamlessly with the game's visuals and mechanics. As technology continues to advance, the possibilities for innovative and immersive game sound design will only expand, offering new ways to engage and captivate players.

Composing Music for Games

Composing music for games is a specialized field that requires a deep understanding of both music and game design. Unlike traditional music composition, game music must adapt to the interactive and dynamic nature of gameplay. This section explores the unique challenges and techniques involved in composing music for games.

One of the primary challenges in game music composition is creating adaptive and dynamic scores. Unlike linear media, where music follows a predetermined path, game music must respond to the player's actions and the game's events in real-time. This requires composers to create modular pieces of music that can be seamlessly combined and altered based on the gameplay context.

A common technique in adaptive music is the use of layered compositions. Composers create multiple layers of music that can be added or removed depending on the game's state. For example, a base layer might provide a calm background, while additional layers can introduce intensity and complexity during combat or high-stress situations. This allows the music to dynamically reflect the game's pacing and emotional tone.

Another technique is the use of musical motifs and themes. By developing recurring musical ideas associated with specific characters, locations, or events, composers can create a cohesive and memorable score. These motifs can be varied and transformed throughout the game to reflect changes in the narrative and character development. For instance, a character's theme might start as a simple melody and evolve into a complex orchestration as they grow and face new challenges.

Interactive music systems are also crucial in game music composition. These systems use algorithms and programming to adjust the music in real-time based on gameplay data. This can include changes in tempo, key, or instrumentation to match the player's actions. For example, entering a new area might trigger a change in music to reflect the environment's mood, or a successful action might be accompanied by a triumphant musical cue.

Collaboration with other game development disciplines is essential for effective game music composition. Composers work closely with designers, programmers, and directors to ensure that the music aligns with the game's vision and enhances the player's experience. This collaboration involves understanding the game's narrative, pacing, and mechanics to create music that supports and enhances these elements.

Technical considerations are also important in game music composition. Music must be optimized for different hardware and software configurations, ensuring consistent quality across various platforms. This includes managing audio compression, implementing spatial audio techniques, and ensuring that the music system performs efficiently within the game's engine.

In addition to these technical and creative challenges, composers must also consider the player's perspective. Game music should enhance immersion without becoming repetitive or intrusive. This requires careful balancing of musical elements and the use of subtle variations to maintain interest. For example, ambient music in exploration sections should provide atmosphere without distracting from the gameplay, while combat music should energize and focus the player without overwhelming them.

Finally, the role of music in storytelling cannot be overstated. Music can convey emotions, highlight narrative moments, and deepen the player's connection to the game's world and characters. By carefully crafting musical cues and themes, composers can enhance the impact of key story events and create a more emotionally resonant experience.

In conclusion, composing music for games is a complex and multifaceted discipline that requires a blend of musical talent, technical knowledge, and collaborative skills. The dynamic and interactive nature of games presents unique challenges and opportunities for composers, allowing them to create innovative and immersive musical experiences. As technology and game design continue to evolve, the possibilities for game music will expand, offering new ways to enhance and enrich the player's journey.

Sound Effects and Audio Immersion

Sound effects are a fundamental component of game audio design, playing a crucial role in creating immersive and engaging experiences. They provide essential feedback, enhance realism, and contribute to the overall atmosphere of the game. This section explores the importance of sound effects and the techniques used to create audio immersion.

One of the primary functions of sound effects is to provide feedback for the player's actions. This can include sounds associated with movement, interactions, and combat. For example, the sound of footsteps varies depending on the surface, providing subtle cues about the environment. The clang of a sword against armor or the explosion of a grenade gives immediate feedback on the player's actions, enhancing the sense of interaction and responsiveness.

Realism is another key aspect of sound effects. Accurate and believable sounds make the game world feel more tangible and immersive. This involves not only the creation of individual sound effects but also their integration into the game environment. Techniques such as spatial audio and reverberation help to place sounds in a three-dimensional space, making them appear as if they are coming from specific locations within the game world.

Spatial audio techniques are essential for creating a sense of depth and directionality. By using binaural or surround sound processing, developers can simulate how sounds interact with the environment and the player's position. This allows players to locate sounds accurately, whether it's the footsteps of an approaching enemy or the distant roar of a dragon. Proper implementation of spatial audio enhances immersion and situational awareness.

Reverberation and echo effects also contribute to audio immersion. These effects simulate how sound waves interact with different surfaces and environments. For example, a gunshot in a confined space will sound different from one in an open field. By adjusting the reverb and echo characteristics, developers can create a more realistic and immersive audio experience.

The creation of sound effects often involves a combination of field recording, Foley techniques, and digital synthesis. Field recording involves capturing real-world sounds, such as footsteps, machinery, or animal noises, which are then processed and integrated into the game. Foley techniques involve creating sound effects in a controlled studio environment, often using props and creative methods to replicate specific sounds. Digital synthesis allows for the creation of unique and fantastical sounds that would be impossible to record in real life.

Interactive sound effects further enhance immersion by responding dynamically to the player's actions and the game's state. For example, the sound of rain might intensify during a storm, or the hum of machinery might change pitch based on the player's proximity. These dynamic sound effects make the game world feel more responsive and alive.

Balancing sound effects with other audio elements is crucial for maintaining clarity and cohesion. In a game with complex audio layers, including music, dialogue, and ambient sounds, it's essential to ensure that sound effects are distinct and appropriately mixed. Techniques such as audio ducking, where the volume of one sound is lowered to make another more prominent, can help achieve this balance.

Sound design also plays a significant role in conveying the game's narrative and emotional tone. Specific sounds can evoke emotions, create tension, or highlight important story moments. For example, the creaking of an old house can create a sense of unease, while the triumphant fanfare after a victory can evoke a sense of accomplishment. By carefully designing and placing sound effects, developers can enhance the storytelling and emotional impact of the game.

In conclusion, sound effects are a vital component of game audio design, contributing to immersion, realism, and player feedback. The techniques used to create and implement sound effects are diverse and complex, requiring a blend of artistic creativity and technical expertise. As audio technology continues to advance, the possibilities for creating immersive and engaging soundscapes in games will expand, offering new ways to enhance the player's experience.

Interactive Audio: Responding to Player Actions

Interactive audio is a defining feature of modern game design, allowing sound to respond dynamically to player actions and game events. This interactivity enhances immersion, making the audio experience unique to each playthrough. This section explores the principles and techniques of interactive audio in games.

One of the core principles of interactive audio is real-time responsiveness. Unlike static audio tracks, interactive audio changes based on the player's actions and the game's state. This can include adaptive music, dynamic sound effects, and responsive dialogue. The goal is to create a seamless audio experience that feels natural and immersive.

Adaptive music is a common feature in interactive audio. It involves creating music that changes in real-time based on the gameplay context. For example, the music might intensify during combat or shift to a more tranquil theme during exploration. This is often achieved through the use of layered compositions, where different musical elements can be added or removed dynamically. By adjusting the intensity, tempo, and instrumentation, adaptive music can reflect the emotional and gameplay dynamics.

Dynamic sound effects respond to the player's actions and the game's environment. For instance, the sound of footsteps may change depending on the surface, or the sound of an explosion may vary based on the player's distance from the source. This responsiveness enhances realism and provides important feedback to the player. Techniques such as procedural audio generation and real-time audio processing are often used to create these dynamic sound effects.

Responsive dialogue systems allow characters to react to the player's choices and actions. This involves recording multiple dialogue variations and using algorithms to select the appropriate response based on the context. For example, an NPC might respond differently based on the player's previous interactions or the current situation. This dynamic dialogue enhances immersion and makes character interactions feel more natural and engaging.

Interactive audio systems often use state-driven approaches to manage audio changes. These systems track the game's state, such as the player's location, actions, and the game's events, and trigger audio changes accordingly. This can involve transitioning between different music tracks, adjusting sound effect parameters, or playing specific dialogue lines. State-driven audio systems ensure that the audio remains coherent and responsive to the gameplay.

Another important aspect of interactive audio is the use of middleware tools. Middleware solutions like FMOD and Wwise provide powerful tools for implementing interactive audio without requiring extensive programming knowledge. These tools allow audio designers to create complex interactive systems, define audio behaviors, and integrate them seamlessly into the game engine. Middleware tools also offer features such as real-time mixing, spatial audio, and adaptive music systems.

The integration of interactive audio requires close collaboration between audio designers, programmers, and other development teams. This collaboration ensures that the audio system aligns with the game's design and enhances the overall experience. Audio designers must work closely with programmers to implement audio triggers, manage audio states, and optimize performance.

Performance optimization is a critical consideration in interactive audio. Real-time audio processing and dynamic changes can be demanding on the system, requiring efficient implementation to maintain performance. This includes managing audio memory, optimizing audio processing, and ensuring that the interactive audio system runs smoothly across different hardware configurations.

In conclusion, interactive audio is a key element of modern game design, providing dynamic and responsive sound that enhances immersion and engagement. By adapting to the player's actions and the game's state, interactive audio creates a unique and personalized audio experience. The techniques and tools used in interactive audio are diverse and complex, requiring a blend of creative and technical skills. As technology continues to advance, the potential for interactive audio will expand, offering new ways to create immersive and engaging soundscapes in games.

The Future of Audio in Games

The future of audio in games promises exciting advancements and innovations, driven by emerging technologies and evolving design practices. As games continue to push the boundaries of interactivity and immersion, audio will play an increasingly significant role in shaping the player experience. This section explores some of the key trends and future possibilities for audio in games.

One of the most significant trends is the advancement of spatial audio technologies. Techniques such as binaural audio, ambisonics, and real-time 3D audio processing are becoming more sophisticated, allowing for highly immersive and realistic soundscapes. These technologies enable precise localization of sounds, creating a sense of depth and directionality that enhances the player's situational awareness and immersion. As VR and AR technologies continue to evolve, spatial audio will become even more crucial in creating believable and engaging virtual environments.

AI and machine learning are also poised to revolutionize game audio. AI-driven audio systems can generate dynamic and contextually appropriate sound effects, music, and dialogue based on player behavior and game events. For example, AI can create adaptive soundscapes that respond to the player's actions, or generate procedural music that evolves in real-time. Machine learning algorithms can also analyze player preferences and tailor the audio experience to individual players, creating a more personalized and immersive experience.

Procedural audio generation is another promising area of development. This technique involves creating sound effects and music algorithmically rather than using pre-recorded samples. Procedural audio can generate highly dynamic and responsive sounds that adapt to the game's environment and player actions. For example, the sound of wind rustling through trees or the noise of a bustling marketplace can be generated in real-time based on environmental variables. Procedural audio offers greater flexibility and variety, reducing the need for extensive sound libraries and enabling more dynamic audio experiences.

Advancements in hardware will also impact the future of game audio. High-fidelity audio hardware, such as advanced headphones and speakers, will provide more accurate and immersive sound reproduction. Innovations in haptic feedback technology, where sound is integrated with tactile sensations, will enhance the sense of immersion by allowing players to feel the audio. These advancements will create more engaging and multisensory experiences.

The integration of audio with other sensory modalities is another exciting possibility. Multisensory experiences that combine audio with visual, haptic, and even olfactory feedback can create deeply immersive and memorable experiences. For example, synchronized audio and haptic feedback can simulate the sensation of firing a weapon or feeling the rumble of an explosion. These multisensory experiences will push the boundaries of immersion and player engagement.

Cloud computing and streaming technologies will also influence the future of game audio. Cloud-based audio processing can offload complex audio tasks from local hardware, allowing for more sophisticated and resource-intensive audio effects. Streaming technologies will enable real-time audio updates and adaptive soundscapes based on live data. These advancements will enhance the flexibility and scalability of game audio, allowing for more dynamic and responsive sound experiences.

In conclusion, the future of audio in games is full of exciting possibilities. Advancements in spatial audio, AI, procedural generation, hardware, and multisensory integration will push the boundaries of what is possible in game audio design. These innovations will create more immersive, dynamic, and personalized audio experiences, enhancing the overall player experience. As technology continues to evolve, audio will play an increasingly important role in shaping the future of games, offering new ways to engage and captivate players.

Chapter 11: AI in Games

The Basics of Game AI

Game AI, or artificial intelligence, refers to the techniques used to create behavior in non-player characters (NPCs) and game environments. The goal is to make these behaviors appear intelligent and lifelike, enhancing the player's experience. Basic AI in games involves pathfinding, decision-making, and pattern recognition.

Pathfinding is the process of determining the optimal route for an NPC to take from one point to another. The most common algorithm used for this purpose is A*, which balances path cost and distance to find efficient routes.

```python
def a_star(start, goal, graph):

open_set = set([start])

closed_set = set()

g = {start: 0}

parents = {start: start}

while open_set:

current = min(open_set, key=lambda node: g[node] + heuristic(node, goal))

if current == goal:

path = []

while parents[current] != current:

path.append(current)

current = parents[current]
```

```
path.append(start)

path.reverse()

return path

open_set.remove(current)

closed_set.add(current)

for neighbor in graph[current]:

if neighbor in closed_set:

continue

if neighbor not in open_set:

open_set.add(neighbor)

tentative_g = g[current] + graph[current][neighbor]

if tentative_g >= g.get(neighbor, float('inf')):

continue

parents[neighbor] = current

g[neighbor] = tentative_g

return None
```

Decision-making involves determining how an NPC should react to various stimuli. Finite State Machines (FSMs) are a simple yet effective way to handle this. An FSM consists of states, transitions, and actions.

Pattern recognition allows NPCs to identify and respond to specific player behaviors. For example, an enemy might recognize a player's tendency to hide and set traps accordingly.

Advanced AI Techniques

Advanced AI techniques go beyond basic behaviors to create more sophisticated and adaptive NPCs. Techniques such as behavior trees, neural networks, and machine learning are often employed.

Behavior trees are a hierarchical model used to control the flow of decision-making in NPCs. They are more flexible than FSMs and allow for complex behaviors through a tree structure of tasks and conditions.

Neural networks, inspired by the human brain, consist of interconnected nodes that process information. They can be trained to recognize patterns and make decisions based on data inputs. In games, neural networks can be used to create NPCs that learn and adapt to the player's style.

Machine learning allows NPCs to improve over time based on their experiences. Reinforcement learning, a subset of machine learning, involves training an NPC to achieve goals through rewards and penalties. This technique can create NPCs that evolve their strategies to become more challenging opponents.

AI-driven Game Design and Player Interaction

AI-driven game design integrates AI techniques into the core design of the game, shaping the player's experience dynamically. Procedural content generation (PCG) is a prime example, where AI algorithms create levels, quests, and environments on-the-fly.

PCG can provide endless variety and replayability. For instance, rogue-like games use PCG to generate unique dungeon layouts for each playthrough. This ensures that players encounter new challenges and surprises every time they play.

AI can also enhance player interaction by creating more responsive and immersive NPCs. Adaptive AI systems can analyze player behavior and adjust the game difficulty accordingly. This creates a balanced and engaging experience for players of all skill levels.

Player modeling involves creating a profile of the player's style, preferences, and skill level. AI can use this model to tailor the game's content and challenges to the individual player. This personalization enhances player engagement and satisfaction.

Ethical Issues in Game AI

The use of AI in games raises several ethical considerations. One major concern is the potential for AI to create addictive gameplay experiences. Game designers must balance creating engaging content with avoiding manipulative practices that exploit players' psychological weaknesses.

Privacy is another concern. Games that collect and analyze player data to drive AI behaviors must ensure that they handle this data responsibly and transparently. Players should be informed about what data is collected and how it is used.

The portrayal of AI-driven characters also poses ethical questions. Developers should strive for inclusive and respectful representations of diverse characters, avoiding stereotypes and harmful tropes.

AI can also be used to enhance accessibility in games. For example, AI-driven assistants can help players with disabilities by adapting controls and providing real-time assistance. This fosters inclusivity and ensures that games are enjoyable for a wider audience.

The Future of AI in Game Development

The future of AI in game development promises exciting advancements. One emerging trend is the use of deep learning, a subset of machine learning, to create more sophisticated AI behaviors. Deep learning models can process vast amounts of data and recognize complex patterns, enabling more realistic and intelligent NPCs.

Another trend is the integration of AI with virtual reality (VR) and augmented reality (AR). AI can enhance the immersion and interactivity of VR/AR experiences by creating responsive and adaptive virtual environments.

AI-driven storytelling is also on the horizon. Future games may feature narratives that evolve based on the player's choices and actions, creating a more personalized and engaging story experience.

Moreover, AI can facilitate the creation of large-scale, open-world games with dynamic ecosystems. NPCs in these games can have their own goals and behaviors, interacting with each other and the player in meaningful ways.

The democratization of AI tools will enable more developers to incorporate advanced AI techniques into their games. This will lead to a broader range of innovative and diverse game experiences.

Chapter 12: User Interface and User Experience

Principles of Game UI/UX Design

User Interface (UI) and User Experience (UX) design are critical aspects of game development that directly impact how players interact with and perceive a game. Effective UI/UX design ensures that players can easily navigate the game, understand its mechanics, and enjoy a seamless experience.

The primary principle of UI/UX design is usability. A game interface should be intuitive, allowing players to focus on gameplay rather than struggling with controls. This involves clear visual hierarchies, consistent design elements, and accessible controls.

Clarity is essential in UI design. Players should be able to quickly understand the purpose of each interface element. This can be achieved through visual cues such as icons, color coding, and tooltips.

Feedback is another crucial principle. The game should provide immediate and clear feedback for player actions. This helps players understand the consequences of their actions and learn the game mechanics. Visual and auditory feedback, such as sound effects and animations, enhance this experience.

Aesthetics play a significant role in UX. The visual style of the UI should match the overall theme of the game, creating a cohesive experience. This includes choosing appropriate fonts, colors, and graphical elements that enhance immersion.

Accessibility is an often-overlooked aspect of UI/UX design. Games should accommodate players with diverse needs, including those with disabilities. This can involve customizable controls, text-to-speech options, and scalable UI elements.

Designing Intuitive Interfaces

Designing intuitive interfaces involves creating layouts and controls that players can easily understand and use. One approach is to follow established design patterns familiar to players. For example, a health bar is typically displayed at the top or bottom of the screen, making it easily recognizable.

Consistency is key in intuitive design. UI elements should behave predictably, allowing players to develop a mental model of how the interface works. This means using the same visual language and interaction patterns throughout the game.

Prototyping and user testing are essential steps in designing intuitive interfaces. By creating wireframes and interactive prototypes, designers can test their concepts with real users and gather feedback. This iterative process helps identify usability issues and refine the design.

Minimizing cognitive load is another important consideration. The interface should present information in a clear and concise manner, avoiding clutter and unnecessary complexity. This helps players focus on important tasks without feeling overwhelmed.

Contextual menus and tooltips can enhance intuitiveness by providing additional information only when needed. This keeps the interface clean while offering guidance to players who seek more details.

Enhancing Player Experience Through Design

Enhancing player experience involves designing UI/UX elements that create a seamless and enjoyable interaction with the game. One way to achieve this is through immersion, where the interface complements the game world rather than distracting from it.

Diegetic interfaces integrate UI elements into the game environment. For example, a holographic map projected from a character's wrist feels more immersive than a traditional on-screen map. This approach blurs the line between gameplay and interface.

Responsive design is another technique to enhance player experience. The interface should adapt to different screen sizes and resolutions, ensuring a consistent experience across various devices. This is especially important for mobile and cross-platform games.

Personalization can greatly enhance player engagement. Allowing players to customize their interface, such as choosing color schemes or rearranging HUD elements, creates a sense of ownership and comfort.

Animation and transitions can make the interface feel more dynamic and responsive. Smooth transitions between menus and subtle animations for button presses add to the overall polish of the game.

UI/UX Challenges in Modern Games

Modern games face several UI/UX challenges due to their increasing complexity and diversity. One major challenge is maintaining clarity in interfaces that need to convey a lot of information, such as in strategy or simulation games.

Balancing aesthetics and functionality is another challenge. While visually striking interfaces can enhance immersion, they must not compromise usability. Striking the right balance requires careful consideration of both design and functionality.

Cross-platform compatibility poses additional challenges. Designing interfaces that work seamlessly on different devices, from PCs to consoles to mobile phones, requires adaptive layouts and control schemes.

Localization and cultural differences also impact UI/UX design. Text, icons, and symbols need to be culturally appropriate and understandable to a global audience. This may involve translating text and adapting visual elements to suit different cultural contexts.

Performance optimization is crucial, especially for resource-intensive games. UI elements should be lightweight and efficient to avoid impacting the game's performance. This includes optimizing assets and minimizing the computational load of animations and effects.

Case Studies: UI/UX Innovations

Several games have pioneered innovative UI/UX designs that set new standards in the industry. For example, "Dead Space" uses a diegetic interface, where health and ammo indicators are integrated into the character's suit. This creates an immersive experience without traditional HUD elements.

"The Witcher 3: Wild Hunt" excels in providing a customizable interface. Players can adjust the HUD to their preferences, hiding or displaying elements as needed. This flexibility enhances the player's control over their experience.

"Journey" is renowned for its minimalistic UI, focusing on intuitive design and visual storytelling. The absence of traditional UI elements directs the player's attention to the environment and interactions, creating a unique and immersive experience.

"Overwatch" incorporates dynamic feedback through visual and auditory cues. The game's UI provides immediate feedback for actions, such as hit markers and sound effects, enhancing player engagement and responsiveness.

"Fortnite" demonstrates effective cross-platform UI design. Its interface adapts seamlessly to various devices, providing a consistent experience whether players are on PC, console, or mobile. This adaptability has contributed to its widespread popularity.

These case studies highlight the importance of innovative and thoughtful UI/UX design in creating engaging and memorable gaming experiences.

Chapter 13: Testing and Quality Assurance

The Importance of Game Testing

Game testing is a critical phase in the development process, ensuring that the final product is both functional and enjoyable for players. Without rigorous testing, games are likely to contain bugs, imbalanced mechanics, and other issues that can detract from the player experience. The primary goal of game testing is to identify and fix these problems before the game is released.

There are several types of testing, each with its own focus and methods. Functional testing ensures that the game works as intended, with all features and mechanics operating correctly. Performance testing evaluates the game's performance under various conditions, such as different hardware configurations and network environments. Usability testing examines the game's interface and controls to ensure they are intuitive and easy to use.

Testing should be conducted continuously throughout the development process, not just at the end. This allows developers to catch and address issues early, reducing the cost and effort required to fix them. Early testing also provides valuable feedback that can inform design decisions and improve the overall quality of the game.

Automated testing tools can be used to perform repetitive tasks and check for common issues, freeing up testers to focus on more complex and nuanced aspects of the game. However, human testers are still essential for identifying subtle bugs, evaluating the player experience, and providing subjective feedback.

Game testing also involves testing for compatibility across different platforms and devices. This ensures that the game performs well on various hardware configurations and operating systems, providing a consistent experience for all players.

Another important aspect of game testing is localization testing, which ensures that the game is properly translated and adapted for different languages and cultures. This includes checking for text overflow, cultural appropriateness, and correct localization of audio and graphical assets.

Testing is a collaborative effort that involves the entire development team. Developers, designers, artists, and testers must work together to identify and fix issues. Clear communication and documentation are essential for coordinating efforts and ensuring that everyone is on the same page.

The testing process should also include feedback from external testers, such as beta testers and focus groups. These testers provide a fresh perspective and can identify issues that the development team may have overlooked. Their feedback is invaluable for refining the game and ensuring that it meets the expectations of its target audience.

In conclusion, game testing is a vital part of the development process that ensures the final product is polished, functional, and enjoyable. By conducting thorough and continuous testing, developers can identify and fix issues early, resulting in a higher quality game that meets the expectations of players.

Methods and Techniques in Game Testing

Game testing involves a variety of methods and techniques, each designed to uncover different types of issues and improve the overall quality of the game. Understanding and implementing these techniques is essential for effective game testing.

One of the most common methods is black box testing, where testers evaluate the game without any knowledge of its internal workings. This approach focuses on the user experience, ensuring that the game functions correctly from the player's perspective. Black box testing can uncover issues with gameplay mechanics, user interface, and overall usability.

White box testing, on the other hand, involves a detailed examination of the game's code and internal structures. Testers with programming knowledge use this method to identify and fix bugs at the code level. White box testing is particularly useful for detecting performance issues, memory leaks, and other technical problems that may not be apparent during gameplay.

Automated testing tools are increasingly used in game testing to perform repetitive tasks and check for common issues. These tools can simulate player actions, test various scenarios, and verify that game elements work as expected. Automated tests can run continuously, providing real-time feedback to developers and helping to catch issues early in the development process.

Exploratory testing is another important technique, where testers play the game without predefined test cases or scripts. This approach allows testers to explore the game freely, uncovering unexpected issues and providing valuable insights into the player experience. Exploratory testing is particularly useful for identifying usability problems, game balance issues, and other subjective aspects of the game.

Regression testing ensures that new updates or changes to the game do not introduce new bugs or break existing functionality. This involves re-running previously conducted tests to verify that the game still works correctly after modifications. Automated regression tests can save time and effort by quickly checking for issues across different game versions.

Load testing evaluates how the game performs under various levels of stress, such as high player traffic or complex in-game scenarios. This is crucial for online multiplayer games, where server stability and performance are essential for a smooth player experience. Load testing helps identify bottlenecks and optimize the game's performance for different environments.

Usability testing focuses on the game's interface and controls, ensuring that they are intuitive and easy to use. Testers observe players as they interact with the game, noting any difficulties or confusion they encounter. This feedback is used to improve the user experience and make the game more accessible to a wider audience.

Compatibility testing ensures that the game works correctly across different platforms, devices, and configurations. This involves testing the game on various hardware and software setups, including different operating systems, graphics cards, and controllers. Compatibility testing helps ensure a consistent and enjoyable experience for all players, regardless of their setup.

Localization testing verifies that the game is properly adapted for different languages and cultures. This includes checking translations, text formatting, audio synchronization, and cultural appropriateness. Localization testing is essential for reaching a global audience and providing a seamless experience for players around the world.

In conclusion, game testing involves a diverse set of methods and techniques, each addressing different aspects of the game. By employing a comprehensive testing strategy, developers can identify and fix issues early, ensuring a high-quality game that meets player expectations.

Balancing and Fine-Tuning Gameplay

Balancing and fine-tuning gameplay is a crucial aspect of game development that ensures a fair, engaging, and enjoyable experience for players. Proper balance involves adjusting various game elements to achieve harmony between challenge and reward, creating a satisfying progression curve and maintaining player interest.

One key aspect of gameplay balance is adjusting difficulty levels. This involves fine-tuning enemy strength, player abilities, resource availability, and other factors to provide an appropriate challenge for players of different skill levels. Developers often use metrics and player feedback to adjust difficulty settings, ensuring that the game remains challenging but not frustrating.

Another important factor is balancing game mechanics. This includes ensuring that no single strategy or playstyle is overwhelmingly powerful, and that all available options are viable and rewarding. Balancing game mechanics requires careful analysis and iteration, often involving playtesting and feedback from a diverse group of players.

Resource management is a critical element in many games, particularly strategy and role-playing games. Balancing resources involves ensuring that players have enough resources to progress without feeling overwhelmed or underpowered. This requires careful consideration of resource generation rates, costs, and rewards.

Player progression is another key area that requires balancing. This includes adjusting experience points, leveling systems, skill trees, and other progression mechanics to provide a satisfying sense of growth and achievement. Developers must ensure that progression is neither too rapid nor too slow, maintaining player engagement throughout the game.

Multiplayer games present unique challenges in balancing gameplay, as developers must ensure fairness and competitiveness between players. This involves adjusting character abilities, weapon strengths, and other gameplay elements to prevent any single player from dominating. Regular updates and patches are often necessary to maintain balance as new strategies and metas emerge.

Data analytics play a significant role in balancing gameplay. By collecting and analyzing player data, developers can identify trends, detect imbalances, and make informed adjustments. Metrics such as win/loss ratios, player progression rates, and in-game economy data provide valuable insights for fine-tuning gameplay.

Feedback from playtesting is essential for balancing gameplay. Developers should conduct playtesting sessions with a diverse group of players, including both experienced gamers and newcomers. This helps identify potential issues and ensures that the game is enjoyable for a wide audience. Playtesting should be an iterative process, with developers making adjustments based on feedback and conducting further tests.

Balancing also involves ensuring that the game's narrative and aesthetics support the gameplay experience. This includes aligning the story, characters, and visuals with the game's mechanics and themes. A cohesive and well-integrated narrative enhances player immersion and satisfaction.

Finally, balancing gameplay requires a flexible and adaptive approach. As players discover new strategies and the game evolves, developers must be willing to make ongoing adjustments. Regular updates, patches, and expansions provide opportunities to refine gameplay balance and address emerging issues.

In conclusion, balancing and fine-tuning gameplay is a complex and iterative process that involves adjusting various game elements to create a fair, engaging, and enjoyable experience. By using data analytics, playtesting, and feedback, developers can achieve a well-balanced game that meets player expectations and maintains long-term interest.

Handling Feedback and Iteration

Handling feedback and iteration is a critical part of the game development process, ensuring that the final product meets player expectations and provides a high-quality experience. Effective feedback management and iterative development help identify and address issues early, refine gameplay, and enhance overall game quality.

Collecting feedback is the first step in this process. Developers can gather feedback from various sources, including playtesters, beta testers, focus groups, and online communities. Each source provides valuable insights into different aspects of the game, from technical performance to gameplay mechanics and user experience.

Structured feedback forms and surveys are useful tools for collecting detailed and specific feedback. These tools can include questions about various aspects of the game, such as controls, graphics, sound, and overall enjoyment. Open-ended questions allow testers to provide more nuanced and subjective feedback.

In addition to structured feedback, developers should also pay attention to unstructured feedback, such as comments on forums, social media, and online reviews. This type of feedback often highlights issues that may not be covered in structured forms and provides a broader perspective on player sentiment.

Once feedback is collected, it must be analyzed and prioritized. Not all feedback is equally important, and developers must determine which issues are most critical to address. This involves evaluating the severity of each issue, the number of players affected, and the potential impact on the overall game experience.

Creating a feedback management system can help organize and track feedback. This system can include a database or spreadsheet where feedback is logged, categorized, and prioritized. Assigning specific team members to handle different types of feedback ensures that all issues are addressed in a timely manner.

Iteration involves making changes to the game based on feedback and then testing those changes. This iterative process allows developers to refine gameplay, fix bugs, and improve overall quality. Iteration should be continuous throughout the development cycle, with regular updates and patches to address new issues as they arise.

Prototyping is an essential part of iteration. Developers can create prototypes of new features or changes to test their impact before fully implementing them. Prototyping helps identify potential problems early and allows for more efficient and effective iteration.

Communication is key during the feedback and iteration process. Developers should maintain open lines of communication with playtesters and the player community, keeping them informed about changes and updates. Transparency helps build trust and encourages players to continue providing valuable feedback.

Collaboration within the development team is also crucial. Developers, designers, artists, and testers must work together to address feedback and make iterative changes. Regular team meetings and discussions ensure that everyone is aligned and working towards the same goals.

Documentation is important for tracking changes and understanding the impact of feedback. Detailed records of feedback, iterations, and updates provide a clear history of the development process and help inform future decisions.

In conclusion, handling feedback and iteration is a vital part of game development that ensures a high-quality final product. By effectively managing feedback, prioritizing issues, and continuously iterating, developers can create a game that meets player expectations and provides an enjoyable experience.

Case Studies: Testing Leading to Success

Case studies of successful game testing highlight the importance of thorough testing and iterative development in producing high-quality games. These examples demonstrate how effective testing processes can identify and resolve issues, enhance gameplay, and ensure a smooth launch.

One notable example is the development of "The Witcher 3: Wild Hunt" by CD Projekt Red. The game's extensive testing phase involved a combination of automated testing, manual playtesting, and feedback from beta testers. The development team conducted numerous playtesting sessions to gather feedback on gameplay mechanics, user interface, and narrative elements. This iterative process allowed them to make necessary adjustments, resulting in a critically acclaimed game that received widespread praise for its depth, storytelling, and polish.

Another successful case is "Overwatch" by Blizzard Entertainment. Blizzard's approach to testing involved a large-scale beta testing phase, where thousands of players were invited to play and provide feedback. The developers used this feedback to fine-tune character balance, gameplay mechanics, and overall game performance. Regular updates and patches were released based on player feedback, ensuring a well-balanced and enjoyable multiplayer experience. The game's success can be attributed to Blizzard's commitment to continuous testing and iteration.

"Naughty Dog's" "The Last of Us" is another excellent example of effective game testing. The development team conducted extensive usability testing to ensure that the game's controls and interface were intuitive and accessible. They also employed a rigorous bug-testing process, utilizing both automated tools and manual testers to identify and fix issues. The result was a game that received critical acclaim for its gameplay, narrative, and emotional impact.

"Destiny 2" by Bungie showcases the importance of post-launch testing and updates. After the game's initial release, the development team continued to gather feedback from players and make iterative improvements. Regular updates addressed balance issues, introduced new content, and enhanced the overall player experience. Bungie's commitment to ongoing testing and iteration helped maintain player engagement and improve the game's long-term success.

Indie game "Hades" by Supergiant Games demonstrates the value of early access testing. The game was released in early access, allowing players to provide feedback throughout the development process. The developers used this feedback to refine gameplay mechanics, adjust difficulty levels, and enhance narrative elements. The iterative development process, driven by player feedback, resulted in a highly polished game that received widespread acclaim upon its full release.

"Fortnite" by Epic Games is a prime example of the importance of performance testing and optimization. The game's massive player base and cross-platform nature required extensive testing to ensure smooth performance across various devices and configurations. Epic Games employed automated testing tools and conducted large-scale stress tests to identify and address performance bottlenecks. Regular updates and optimizations helped maintain a stable and enjoyable experience for players.

In conclusion, these case studies highlight the critical role of testing and iteration in game development. By gathering feedback, conducting thorough testing, and making iterative improvements, developers can create high-quality games that meet player expectations and achieve commercial success.

Chapter 14: The Business of Game Development

Overview of the Game Industry

The game industry is a dynamic and rapidly evolving sector, encompassing a wide range of activities from game development and publishing to marketing and distribution. Understanding the structure and trends of the game industry is crucial for anyone looking to enter or succeed in this field.

The industry can be broadly divided into several key segments: developers, publishers, distributors, and retailers. Developers are responsible for creating games, including designing, programming, and testing. Publishers finance and market games, often taking on the role of distributing and selling the final product. Distributors handle the logistics of getting games from developers or publishers to retailers, who then sell the games to consumers.

The game industry has seen significant growth over the past few decades, driven by advancements in technology and the increasing popularity of gaming as a form of entertainment. The rise of digital distribution platforms, such as Steam, the PlayStation Store, and the Xbox Marketplace, has transformed how games are sold and consumed. These platforms allow developers to reach a global audience with minimal physical distribution costs.

Mobile gaming has emerged as a major segment of the industry, with smartphones and tablets becoming popular gaming devices. The accessibility and convenience of mobile games have attracted a broad and diverse audience, contributing to the industry's growth. Free-to-play models, supported by in-game purchases and advertisements, have become a prevalent business model in mobile gaming.

The rise of esports has also had a significant impact on the game industry. Competitive gaming has grown into a global phenomenon, with professional players, teams, and tournaments attracting millions of viewers and substantial sponsorship deals. Esports has opened up new revenue streams for developers and publishers, including broadcasting rights, merchandise sales, and event sponsorships.

Virtual reality (VR) and augmented reality (AR) technologies are emerging trends that have the potential to reshape the game industry. VR and AR offer immersive gaming experiences that were previously unimaginable, and their continued development is likely to create new opportunities and challenges for developers.

The game industry is also characterized by a high level of innovation and creativity. Developers are constantly exploring new genres, gameplay mechanics, and storytelling techniques to create unique and engaging experiences. This drive for innovation has led to the creation of indie games, which often push the boundaries of traditional game design and offer fresh perspectives.

However, the game industry also faces several challenges. The high cost of game development, especially for AAA titles, can be a significant barrier for new entrants. Competition is fierce, and the market is crowded with numerous games vying for players' attention. Additionally, issues such as crunch culture, diversity and inclusion, and ethical concerns around monetization practices are ongoing challenges that the industry must address.

In conclusion, the game industry is a complex and multifaceted sector with significant opportunities and challenges. Understanding the industry's structure, trends, and dynamics is essential for anyone looking to navigate this exciting and ever-changing field.

Starting a Game Development Business

Starting a game development business requires careful planning, a clear vision, and a thorough understanding of the industry. Aspiring game developers must consider various factors, from forming a team to securing funding and navigating the competitive market.

The first step in starting a game development business is defining your vision and goals. This includes identifying the type of games you want to create, your target audience, and your unique selling points. A clear vision will guide your decision-making process and help you stay focused on your objectives.

Forming a skilled and dedicated team is crucial for the success of your game development business. Depending on the size and scope of your projects, your team may include programmers, designers, artists, writers, and marketing professionals. It's essential to find individuals who are not only talented but also share your passion and vision for game development.

Creating a business plan is a vital step in establishing your game development business. Your business plan should outline your goals, target audience, budget, timeline, and marketing strategy. It should also include a detailed financial plan, projecting your expenses, revenue, and potential funding sources. A well-crafted business plan will serve as a roadmap for your business and help attract investors and partners.

Securing funding is one of the biggest challenges for new game development businesses. There are several potential sources of funding, including personal savings, loans, angel investors, venture capital, and crowdfunding. Each funding source has its advantages and disadvantages, and it's essential to choose the one that best suits your needs and goals.

Once you have secured funding, you can start developing your game. This involves several stages, including concept development, prototyping, production, testing, and launch. It's crucial to follow a structured development process, ensuring that each stage is completed thoroughly before moving on to the next.

Marketing is a critical aspect of starting a game development business. Building awareness and generating interest in your game is essential for attracting players and generating sales. This involves creating a marketing plan that includes strategies for social media, public relations, influencer partnerships, and paid advertising. It's also important to engage with your community, gathering feedback and building a loyal fanbase.

Legal considerations are another important aspect of starting a game development business. This includes registering your business, protecting your intellectual property, and complying with industry regulations. It's advisable to consult with legal professionals to ensure that all legal aspects are properly addressed.

Networking and building relationships within the industry can also benefit your game development business. Attending industry events, joining professional organizations, and participating in online forums can help you connect with other developers, publishers, and potential partners. These connections can provide valuable insights, support, and opportunities for collaboration.

Launching your game is a significant milestone, but it's not the end of the journey. Post-launch support, including updates, bug fixes, and new content, is essential for maintaining player engagement and satisfaction. Gathering feedback from players and continuously improving your game can lead to long-term success.

In conclusion, starting a game development business requires careful planning, a clear vision, and a dedicated team. By following a structured approach and addressing key considerations such as funding, marketing, and legal aspects, you can establish a successful game development business and create engaging and memorable games.

Funding and Investment in Game Projects

Funding and investment are critical components of game development, enabling developers to bring their creative visions to life. Securing the necessary financial resources can be challenging, but understanding the various funding options and strategies can help developers navigate this crucial aspect of the industry.

Personal savings and bootstrapping are common initial funding sources for many independent developers. Using personal funds allows developers to maintain complete control over their projects without the pressure of external investors. However, this approach can be risky, as it relies heavily on the developer's financial stability and may limit the scope of the project.

Loans from banks or financial institutions are another option for funding game projects. These loans provide the necessary capital to start development but come with the obligation to repay the borrowed amount with interest. Developers need a solid business plan and financial projections to secure a loan, and they must be prepared to manage the debt responsibly.

Angel investors and venture capitalists are potential sources of significant funding for game projects. Angel investors are typically wealthy individuals who invest their own money in exchange for equity in the company. Venture capitalists, on the other hand, manage large pools of capital from various investors and seek high returns on their investments. Both options provide substantial funding but require developers to give up a portion of ownership and control.

Crowdfunding has become a popular method for funding game projects, particularly for independent developers. Platforms like Kickstarter, Indiegogo, and Patreon allow developers to raise funds directly from their future players and fans. Successful crowdfunding campaigns not only provide financial resources but also help build a community of supporters and generate early interest in the game. However, running a successful campaign requires careful planning, effective marketing, and clear communication with backers.

Grants and subsidies from government agencies, industry organizations, and private foundations can provide funding without requiring repayment or equity. These grants are often awarded based on the project's potential impact, innovation, and cultural significance. Developers must submit detailed proposals and compete with other applicants to secure these funds.

Publisher funding is another common method of financing game projects. Publishers provide financial resources, marketing support, and distribution channels in exchange for a share of the game's revenue. This partnership allows developers to focus on development while leveraging the publisher's expertise and resources. However, it often involves giving up some creative control and sharing profits.

Investment from larger game companies or strategic partners can also be a viable funding option. These partnerships can provide not only financial support but also access to valuable resources, technology, and expertise. Developers must carefully negotiate the terms of these partnerships to ensure they align with their long-term goals and vision.

Revenue from early access sales and pre-orders can provide additional funding during the development process. Offering early access to the game allows developers to generate income, gather player feedback, and build a community before the official launch. Pre-order campaigns can also generate funds and gauge market interest, providing valuable insights for finalizing the game's development and marketing strategies.

In conclusion, funding and investment are critical for game development, and developers have several options to consider. By understanding the advantages and challenges of each funding source, developers can make informed decisions and secure the necessary resources to bring their projects to life.

Marketing and Selling Your Game

Marketing and selling your game are crucial steps in ensuring its success and reaching your target audience. A well-executed marketing strategy can generate interest, build a community, and drive sales, ultimately determining the game's commercial performance.

The first step in marketing your game is to identify your target audience. Understanding who your potential players are, their preferences, and where they spend their time online will help you tailor your marketing efforts effectively. Conducting market research, analyzing similar games, and gathering feedback from early playtests can provide valuable insights into your target audience.

Creating a compelling brand identity for your game is essential for standing out in a crowded market. This includes designing a memorable logo, selecting a distinctive art style, and developing a unique voice and tone for your marketing materials. Consistent branding across all channels helps create a strong and recognizable presence that resonates with your audience.

Building a website for your game is a crucial component of your marketing strategy. Your website should serve as a central hub for all information about your game, including features, release dates, trailers, and press kits. It should also provide a way for potential players to sign up for newsletters, follow your social media channels, and participate in community forums.

Social media marketing is a powerful tool for reaching and engaging with your audience. Platforms like Twitter, Facebook, Instagram, and TikTok allow you to share updates, behind-the-scenes content, and engage with your community. Regularly posting content, responding to comments, and participating in relevant discussions can help build a loyal following and generate buzz around your game.

Influencer partnerships can amplify your marketing efforts and reach a wider audience. Collaborating with popular streamers, YouTubers, and social media influencers who align with your game's genre and style can generate valuable exposure and credibility. Influencers can create gameplay videos, reviews, and live streams, showcasing your game to their followers and driving interest and sales.

Press coverage is another important aspect of marketing your game. Reaching out to gaming journalists, bloggers, and media outlets with press releases, review copies, and exclusive content can generate valuable publicity. Building relationships with the press and providing them with high-quality assets and information increases the likelihood of your game being featured in articles, reviews, and industry news.

Participating in industry events, such as game conventions, trade shows, and online expos, provides opportunities to showcase your game to a broader audience. These events allow you to network with industry professionals, gather feedback from players, and generate media coverage. Having a strong presence at these events can create buzz and attract potential players and partners.

Paid advertising can complement your organic marketing efforts and reach a broader audience. This includes running ads on social media platforms, search engines, and gaming websites. Targeted advertising allows you to reach specific demographics, interests, and behaviors, ensuring that your ads are seen by potential players who are most likely to be interested in your game.

Community engagement is essential for building a loyal player base and generating word-of-mouth marketing. Creating and moderating online communities, such as Discord servers, Reddit forums, and Facebook groups, allows you to interact with your players, gather feedback, and provide support. Encouraging player-generated content, such as fan art, mods, and gameplay videos, can further enhance community engagement and spread awareness of your game.

In conclusion, marketing and selling your game requires a comprehensive and multi-faceted approach. By identifying your target audience, building a strong brand, leveraging social media, influencers, press, events, and paid advertising, and engaging with your community, you can effectively promote your game and drive its commercial success.

Navigating the Challenges of the Game Industry

Navigating the challenges of the game industry requires resilience, adaptability, and a strategic approach. The industry is highly competitive and constantly evolving, presenting both opportunities and obstacles for developers and businesses.

One of the primary challenges is the high cost of game development. Creating a high-quality game requires significant financial resources for talent, technology, marketing, and distribution. Managing budgets effectively and securing adequate funding are crucial for sustaining development and achieving commercial success.

The competitive nature of the game industry is another major challenge. With thousands of games released each year, standing out in a crowded market can be difficult. Developing a unique and compelling game concept, combined with effective marketing strategies, is essential for attracting attention and gaining a competitive edge.

Crunch culture, characterized by extended periods of intense work and overtime, is a pervasive issue in the game industry. While crunch can lead to burnout, decreased productivity, and negative impacts on mental health, it is often seen as necessary to meet tight deadlines. Addressing crunch culture requires fostering a healthy work environment, setting realistic timelines, and prioritizing work-life balance.

Diversity and inclusion are ongoing challenges in the game industry. Ensuring diverse representation in game development teams and creating inclusive games that reflect a broad range of experiences and perspectives is essential for reaching a wider audience and fostering innovation. This involves actively promoting diversity in hiring, addressing biases, and creating supportive workplace cultures.

Monetization practices, such as microtransactions, loot boxes, and in-game purchases, have sparked ethical concerns and regulatory scrutiny. Balancing revenue generation with fair and transparent monetization strategies is crucial for maintaining player trust and satisfaction. Developers must navigate these challenges by implementing ethical practices and complying with regulations.

Intellectual property (IP) protection is another important consideration. Protecting your game's IP from infringement and piracy is essential for safeguarding your investment and ensuring fair competition. This involves securing trademarks, copyrights, and patents, as well as monitoring and addressing unauthorized use of your IP.

Rapid technological advancements and changing consumer preferences require developers to stay adaptable and forward-thinking. Keeping up with emerging trends, such as virtual reality, augmented reality, cloud gaming, and artificial intelligence, is essential for staying competitive and meeting player expectations. This involves continuous learning, experimentation, and investment in new technologies.

Building and maintaining a positive reputation is crucial for long-term success in the game industry. Delivering high-quality games, providing excellent customer support, and engaging with the player community can enhance your reputation and build brand loyalty. Addressing negative feedback and issues transparently and promptly is also important for maintaining player trust.

Regulatory compliance is another challenge that developers must navigate. This includes adhering to laws and regulations related to data privacy, consumer protection, accessibility, and age ratings. Ensuring compliance requires staying informed about relevant regulations, implementing necessary safeguards, and seeking legal advice when needed.

Finally, managing growth and scalability is a significant challenge for successful game development businesses. As your business grows, you must manage increased demands on resources, talent, and infrastructure. This involves strategic planning, efficient resource allocation, and building scalable processes and systems to support growth.

In conclusion, navigating the challenges of the game industry requires a strategic and adaptable approach. By addressing issues such as high development costs, competition, crunch culture, diversity, monetization, IP protection, technological advancements, reputation management, regulatory compliance, and scalability, developers can position themselves for long-term success in this dynamic and evolving industry.

Case Studies: Testing Leading to Success

Case studies of successful game testing highlight the importance of thorough testing and iterative development in producing high-quality games. These examples demonstrate how effective testing processes can identify and resolve issues, enhance gameplay, and ensure a smooth launch.

One notable example is the development of "The Witcher 3: Wild Hunt" by CD Projekt Red. The game's extensive testing phase involved a combination of automated testing, manual playtesting, and feedback from beta testers. The development team conducted numerous playtesting sessions to gather feedback on gameplay mechanics, user interface, and narrative elements. This iterative process allowed them to make necessary adjustments, resulting in a critically acclaimed game that received widespread praise for its depth, storytelling, and polish.

Another successful case is "Overwatch" by Blizzard Entertainment. Blizzard's approach to testing involved a large-scale beta testing phase, where thousands of players were invited to play and provide feedback. The developers used this feedback to fine-tune character balance, gameplay mechanics, and overall game performance. Regular updates and patches were released based on player feedback, ensuring a well-balanced and enjoyable multiplayer experience. The game's success can be attributed to Blizzard's commitment to continuous testing and iteration.

"Naughty Dog's" "The Last of Us" is another excellent example of effective game testing. The development team conducted extensive usability testing to ensure that the game's controls and interface were intuitive and accessible. They also employed a rigorous bug-testing process, utilizing both automated tools and manual testers to identify and fix issues. The result was a game that received critical acclaim for its gameplay, narrative, and emotional impact.

"Destiny 2" by Bungie showcases the importance of post-launch testing and updates. After the game's initial release, the development team continued to gather feedback from players and make iterative improvements. Regular updates addressed balance issues, introduced new content, and enhanced the overall player experience. Bungie's commitment to ongoing testing and iteration helped maintain player engagement and improve the game's long-term success.

Indie game "Hades" by Supergiant Games demonstrates the value of early access testing. The game was released in early access, allowing players to provide feedback throughout the development process. The developers used this feedback to refine gameplay mechanics, adjust difficulty levels, and enhance narrative elements. The iterative development process, driven by player feedback, resulted in a highly polished game that received widespread acclaim upon its full release.

"Fortnite" by Epic Games is a prime example of the importance of performance testing and optimization. The game's massive player base and cross-platform nature required extensive testing to ensure smooth performance across various devices and configurations. Epic Games employed automated testing tools and conducted large-scale stress tests to identify and address performance bottlenecks. Regular updates and optimizations helped maintain a stable and enjoyable experience for players.

In conclusion, these case studies highlight the critical role of testing and iteration in game development. By gathering feedback, conducting thorough testing, and making iterative improvements, developers can create high-quality games that meet player expectations and achieve commercial success.

Chapter 15: Cultural Impact of Games

Games as Cultural Artifacts

Games have evolved from mere entertainment to significant cultural artifacts that reflect and influence society. As cultural artifacts, games encapsulate the values, norms, and ideologies of the societies that produce them. They serve as a medium for storytelling, artistic expression, and social commentary, much like literature, film, and music.

The design and content of games often reflect contemporary issues, such as politics, gender roles, and social justice. For instance, games like "Papers, Please" and "This War of Mine" provide commentary on immigration policies and the human cost of war, respectively. These games engage players in complex ethical dilemmas and encourage them to reflect on real-world issues.

Moreover, games preserve cultural narratives and traditions. Many games incorporate folklore, mythology, and historical events, making them a tool for cultural preservation and education. Games like "Assassin's Creed" series, which are set in meticulously recreated historical periods, offer players an immersive way to experience history and learn about different cultures.

Games also serve as a platform for cultural exchange. In the globalized world, games developed in one culture can be played and appreciated by people worldwide. This cross-cultural interaction can foster greater understanding and appreciation of diverse cultures. For example, Japanese games like "Final Fantasy" and "The Legend of Zelda" have gained immense popularity worldwide, introducing players to aspects of Japanese culture and aesthetics.

Furthermore, the cultural impact of games extends to language and communication. Terms and phrases from popular games often enter the vernacular, influencing how people speak and interact. The concept of "leveling up" or "boss fight" has transcended gaming and is now commonly used in everyday language to describe overcoming challenges or achieving personal growth.

In addition to their cultural significance, games have a profound impact on identity formation. Players often identify with the characters they play, and the virtual worlds they inhabit can influence their perceptions of themselves and others. Games provide a space for exploring different identities and experiences, which can be particularly valuable for marginalized communities.

The cultural impact of games is also evident in the rise of game-related events and communities. Conventions like E3 and PAX, as well as esports tournaments, attract millions of attendees and viewers, showcasing the cultural importance of games. These events foster a sense of community among gamers and provide a platform for discussing and celebrating game culture.

As cultural artifacts, games also reflect and shape technological advancements. The development of new gaming technologies, such as virtual reality (VR) and augmented reality (AR), has cultural implications, influencing how people perceive and interact with the world. These technologies are pushing the boundaries of storytelling and immersion, offering new ways to experience and interpret culture.

The cultural impact of games is multifaceted and far-reaching. They are not only a source of entertainment but also a medium for cultural expression, preservation, and exchange. As games continue to evolve, their role as cultural artifacts will undoubtedly grow, offering new opportunities for understanding and shaping the world around us.

Analyzing the Cultural Influence of Games

Analyzing the cultural influence of games involves examining how they reflect, shape, and challenge societal norms and values. Games are a mirror of society, often depicting and responding to cultural trends, political climates, and social issues. This analysis can be approached from various perspectives, including sociological, psychological, and anthropological.

From a sociological perspective, games can be seen as a reflection of social structures and power dynamics. They often depict societal hierarchies, norms, and roles, providing insights into how these elements are perceived and constructed. For example, the representation of gender roles in games has been a topic of much discussion and critique. Games like "Tomb Raider" and "The Last of Us" have been analyzed for their portrayal of female protagonists, offering both progressive and stereotypical representations.

Psychologically, games influence and are influenced by players' behaviors and attitudes. They provide a space for exploring identity, morality, and social interaction. Research has shown that games can impact players' empathy, aggression, and problem-solving skills. For instance, role-playing games (RPGs) that involve moral decision-making can enhance players' understanding of ethical dilemmas and empathy towards others.

Anthropologically, games can be studied as cultural artifacts that embody the rituals, myths, and values of the cultures that create them. They often incorporate elements of folklore, religion, and history, providing a rich source of material for cultural analysis. Games like "Okami" and "God of War" draw heavily from Japanese and Norse mythology, respectively, offering players an immersive experience of these cultural narratives.

The cultural influence of games extends beyond their content to their production and consumption. The game development industry is itself a cultural phenomenon, with its own norms, practices, and economic structures. The rise of indie games, for instance, reflects a cultural shift towards valuing creativity and innovation over commercial success. Indie games often tackle unconventional themes and experimental gameplay, challenging mainstream gaming norms.

Consumption patterns of games also offer insights into cultural trends. The popularity of certain genres, themes, or mechanics can indicate broader societal interests and concerns. For example, the surge in popularity of survival games like "Minecraft" and "Fortnite" can be seen as a reflection of contemporary anxieties about survival, resource management, and social cooperation.

Furthermore, the cultural influence of games is evident in the communities they create. Online gaming communities, forums, and social media platforms are spaces where players share experiences, discuss game content, and form social bonds. These communities often develop their own cultures, with unique norms, languages, and traditions. The phenomenon of "modding," where players create custom content for games, is an example of how players actively contribute to and shape game culture.

The cultural analysis of games also involves examining their impact on other media and art forms. Games have influenced film, literature, and music, contributing to the creation of transmedia narratives and cross-media collaborations. Movies based on games, like the "Resident Evil" series, and novels inspired by game worlds, such as "The Witcher" series, demonstrate the cultural permeation of game narratives.

Analyzing the cultural influence of games provides valuable insights into how they shape and are shaped by society. It highlights the dynamic relationship between games and culture, revealing the ways in which games reflect, challenge, and contribute to the ongoing dialogue about societal values, norms, and identities.

Games in Education and Training

Games have increasingly been recognized for their potential in education and training. Their interactive and immersive nature makes them powerful tools for learning, providing engaging and effective educational experiences. The application of games in education spans various fields, from K-12 education to professional training and beyond.

In K-12 education, games are used to teach a wide range of subjects, including mathematics, science, history, and language arts. Educational games like "Minecraft: Education Edition" and "Kerbal Space Program" offer students hands-on, experiential learning opportunities. These games help develop critical thinking, problem-solving, and creativity by allowing students to experiment, explore, and build in a virtual environment.

The use of games in education is supported by theories of active learning and constructivism, which emphasize the importance of engaging learners in meaningful, interactive experiences. Games provide immediate feedback and adapt to the learner's level, offering personalized learning experiences that traditional educational methods often lack. This adaptability makes games particularly effective for differentiated instruction, where students with varying abilities and learning styles can benefit from tailored educational content.

In higher education, games are used to simulate complex systems and scenarios, providing students with practical experience in a controlled environment. For example, medical schools use simulation games to train students in surgical procedures and patient care. These simulations allow students to practice and refine their skills without the risk associated with real-life scenarios. Similarly, business schools use management and strategy games to teach students about organizational behavior, decision-making, and market dynamics.

Professional training also benefits from the use of games. In fields such as military, aviation, and emergency response, simulation games provide realistic training environments that enhance skills and preparedness. These games replicate real-world challenges and scenarios, allowing trainees to practice responses and develop critical skills in a safe and controlled setting. For instance, pilots use flight simulators to train for various flight conditions and emergencies, improving their proficiency and confidence.

The effectiveness of games in education and training is supported by research indicating that they can enhance motivation, engagement, and retention of information. Games make learning enjoyable and motivating, encouraging learners to persist in their efforts and achieve mastery. The immersive nature of games also helps learners retain information better by creating memorable and meaningful learning experiences.

Moreover, games foster collaboration and social learning. Many educational games are designed for multiplayer interactions, where learners work together to achieve common goals. This collaborative aspect of gaming promotes teamwork, communication, and social skills, which are essential in both educational and professional settings. For example, games like "Keep Talking and Nobody Explodes" require players to communicate effectively and solve problems together, enhancing their collaborative skills.

The integration of games into education and training also aligns with the growing emphasis on digital literacy. As digital technologies become increasingly prevalent, developing digital literacy skills is crucial. Games, as a form of digital media, provide opportunities for learners to develop these skills, including navigating digital environments, using digital tools, and understanding digital content.

In conclusion, games offer significant potential for enhancing education and training. Their interactive, immersive, and engaging nature makes them effective tools for learning, providing meaningful and personalized educational experiences. As the use of games in education continues to grow, it is important to explore and understand their impact, ensuring that they are used effectively and ethically to support learning and development.

The Globalization of Game Culture

The globalization of game culture refers to the spread and influence of gaming practices, norms, and content across different cultures and regions. This phenomenon has been facilitated by the proliferation of digital technologies, the internet, and the global reach of the gaming industry. The globalization of game culture has significant implications for cultural exchange, identity, and diversity.

One of the key aspects of the globalization of game culture is the widespread accessibility of games. With the advent of digital distribution platforms like Steam, PlayStation Network, and Xbox Live, games developed in one part of the world can be easily accessed and played by people globally. This has led to the dissemination of gaming practices and norms, as players from different cultures engage with and influence each other.

The globalization of game culture also involves the cross-cultural exchange of game content and aesthetics. Games often incorporate elements from different cultures, creating a fusion of styles and themes. For example, games like "Sekiro: Shadows Die Twice" blend Japanese samurai culture with fantasy elements, appealing to a global audience. Similarly, games like "The Witcher 3: Wild

Hunt" draw from Slavic mythology and folklore, introducing players worldwide to these cultural narratives.

This cross-cultural exchange is further facilitated by the internet and social media, where players share experiences, discuss games, and form communities. Online forums, streaming platforms, and social media groups provide spaces for gamers from different parts of the world to interact and connect. These interactions contribute to the creation of a global gaming culture, where players share common interests, values, and practices.

The globalization of game culture also has implications for identity formation and representation. As games reach a global audience, the representation of diverse cultures and identities becomes increasingly important. Players from different backgrounds seek to see themselves reflected in the games they play. This has led to a growing demand for diverse and inclusive representation in games, prompting developers to create characters and stories that reflect a wider range of experiences and identities.

However, the globalization of game culture also raises challenges related to cultural sensitivity and appropriation. The incorporation of cultural elements in games must be done respectfully and accurately, avoiding stereotypes and misrepresentations. Developers need to engage with and understand the cultures they depict, ensuring that their portrayals are authentic and respectful. This requires collaboration with cultural experts and communities, as well as a commitment to ethical representation.

The economic impact of the globalization of game culture is significant. The gaming industry has become a major global economic force, with markets in Asia, North America, and Europe driving its growth. The success of games in different regions reflects the diverse tastes and preferences of players worldwide. For example, mobile games are particularly popular in Asia, while console and PC games dominate in Western markets. Understanding these regional differences is crucial for developers seeking to succeed in the global market.

Furthermore, the globalization of game culture has led to the rise of esports, which has become a global phenomenon. Esports tournaments attract participants and viewers from around the world, showcasing the competitive and communal aspects of gaming. These events highlight the global nature of game culture, as players and fans from different cultures come together to celebrate their shared passion for gaming.

In conclusion, the globalization of game culture is a complex and multifaceted phenomenon. It involves the spread and exchange of gaming practices, norms, and content across different cultures, facilitated by digital technologies and the internet. This has significant implications for cultural exchange, identity, and diversity, as well as economic and social dynamics. As game culture continues to globalize, it is important to navigate these dynamics thoughtfully and ethically, ensuring that games contribute positively to the cultural landscape.

Addressing Cultural Sensitivity in Games

Addressing cultural sensitivity in games involves ensuring that games are inclusive, respectful, and accurate in their portrayal of different cultures and identities. This is crucial for creating games that resonate with diverse audiences and contribute positively to cultural understanding and representation. Developers need to be mindful of cultural nuances and avoid perpetuating stereotypes or misrepresentations.

One of the first steps in addressing cultural sensitivity is conducting thorough research. Developers should engage with the cultures they depict, understanding their history, values, and traditions. This involves consulting cultural experts, historians, and members of the community to ensure that the portrayal is accurate and respectful. For example, when creating a game set in a specific historical period, developers should collaborate with historians to ensure that the depiction is authentic and free from anachronisms.

Another important aspect of cultural sensitivity is representation. Games should reflect the diversity of the real world, offering a range of characters and narratives that represent different cultures, genders, and identities. This not only makes games more inclusive but also enriches the gaming experience by providing players with varied perspectives and stories. Developers should strive to create characters that are multidimensional and avoid relying on stereotypes or clichés.

Inclusivity in game development also involves considering the accessibility of games for players from different backgrounds. This includes providing language options, accommodating different cultural norms and practices, and ensuring that games are playable and enjoyable for people with disabilities. For example, games should offer subtitles and audio descriptions for players with hearing or visual impairments, and consider cultural differences in gameplay mechanics and themes.

Ethical considerations are also paramount in addressing cultural sensitivity. Developers should be aware of the potential impact of their games on players and society. This involves avoiding content that could be offensive or harmful, such as hate speech, violence, or discrimination. Games should promote positive values and respect for all cultures and identities, fostering an environment of inclusivity and understanding.

Furthermore, addressing cultural sensitivity involves being open to feedback and willing to make changes. Developers should listen to the concerns and suggestions of players and communities, using this feedback to improve their games. This iterative process ensures that games continue to evolve and become more inclusive and respectful over time. For example, if a game receives criticism for its portrayal of a particular culture, developers should engage with the community, understand their concerns, and make necessary adjustments to the game.

In addition to internal efforts, the industry as a whole needs to prioritize cultural sensitivity. This includes creating policies and guidelines for inclusive game development, providing training for developers on cultural competence, and promoting diversity within the industry. Organizations and associations can play a crucial role in advocating for these practices and supporting developers in creating culturally sensitive games.

The role of media and critics is also important in addressing cultural sensitivity. Reviews and critiques can highlight issues of representation and inclusivity, raising awareness and encouraging developers to consider these aspects in their work. Constructive criticism can guide developers towards more ethical and respectful portrayals, ultimately contributing to the creation of better games.

In conclusion, addressing cultural sensitivity in games is essential for creating inclusive, respectful, and engaging gaming experiences. It requires a commitment to research, representation, ethical considerations, and openness to feedback. By prioritizing cultural sensitivity, developers can contribute to a more inclusive and diverse gaming landscape, fostering greater understanding and appreciation of different cultures and identities.

Chapter 16: Ethical Game Design

Ethics in Game Development

Ethics in game development is a critical consideration that encompasses a range of issues, from content creation and representation to business practices and player well-being. As games become more influential and pervasive, developers have a responsibility to ensure that their work adheres to ethical standards and contributes positively to society.

One of the primary ethical concerns in game development is the portrayal of violence. While many games feature violent content, it is important to consider how this violence is depicted and its potential impact on players. Developers should avoid gratuitous violence and ensure that violent content serves a meaningful purpose within the game's narrative. Research has shown that excessive exposure to violent media can desensitize individuals to real-world violence, making it crucial to handle such content responsibly.

Another significant ethical issue is representation and inclusivity. Games should strive to represent a diverse range of characters and narratives, avoiding stereotypes and clichés. This involves creating characters that reflect different genders, ethnicities, sexual orientations, and abilities in a respectful and accurate manner. Inclusive representation not only enriches the gaming experience but also helps to combat prejudice and promote empathy.

The ethical implications of game mechanics and design choices are also important. For instance, the use of loot boxes and microtransactions has been widely criticized for encouraging gambling-like behavior, particularly among young players. Developers should consider the potential harm of these mechanics and explore alternative monetization strategies that do not exploit players. Transparency and fairness in game design are essential to maintaining player trust and well-being.

Privacy and data security are critical ethical considerations in the digital age. Games often collect and process personal data from players, making it imperative to handle this information responsibly. Developers should implement robust data protection measures and ensure that players are informed about how their data is used. Respecting players' privacy and obtaining their consent for data collection are fundamental ethical obligations.

The working conditions within the game development industry also raise ethical concerns. Reports of crunch time, where developers work excessively long hours to meet deadlines, highlight the need for better labor practices. Ethical game development involves ensuring fair treatment, reasonable working hours, and a healthy work-life balance for all employees. Sustainable working conditions not only benefit developers but also lead to better-quality games.

Furthermore, ethical game development includes considering the environmental impact of game production and distribution. The gaming industry, like many others, has a carbon footprint that can be reduced through sustainable practices. This involves minimizing waste, using renewable energy sources, and promoting digital distribution over physical copies to reduce the environmental impact.

The social impact of games is another important ethical consideration. Games have the power to influence attitudes and behaviors, making it crucial to consider their potential effects on society. Developers should aim to create games that promote positive values, such as cooperation, empathy, and critical thinking. Games can also be used as tools for education and social change, addressing important issues like climate change, mental health, and social justice.

Transparency and honesty in marketing and communication are also key ethical principles. Developers should provide accurate information about their games, avoiding misleading claims and hype. Honest communication helps build trust with players and ensures that they have realistic expectations about the game.

In conclusion, ethics in game development is a multifaceted issue that requires careful consideration and responsible action. By prioritizing ethical standards, developers can create games that are not only entertaining but also contribute positively to society. This involves addressing issues of violence, representation, game mechanics, privacy, working conditions, environmental impact, social influence, and transparency. Ethical game development ultimately benefits players, developers, and society as a whole.

Responsible Representation in Games

Responsible representation in games involves creating characters, narratives, and environments that accurately and respectfully reflect the diversity of the real world. This includes considering gender, ethnicity, sexual orientation, ability, and other aspects of identity in a way that avoids stereotypes and promotes inclusivity. Responsible representation is essential for creating games that resonate with a diverse audience and contribute positively to cultural understanding.

One of the key aspects of responsible representation is avoiding stereotypes and clichés. Stereotypes are oversimplified and often negative representations of particular groups that can perpetuate prejudice and misunderstanding. For example, depicting female characters solely as damsels in distress or overly sexualized figures reinforces harmful gender stereotypes. Instead, developers should strive to create multidimensional characters with complex personalities, motivations, and roles.

Inclusivity in character design also means representing a wide range of identities. This involves including characters from different ethnic backgrounds, genders, sexual orientations, and abilities. Representation should be thoughtful and intentional, ensuring that characters are portrayed in a way that is respectful and accurate. For instance, including characters with disabilities in meaningful roles can challenge societal perceptions and promote empathy and understanding.

Consultation and collaboration with communities are crucial for responsible representation. Developers should engage with individuals and groups from the communities they are representing to ensure authenticity and respect. This can involve hiring cultural consultants, conducting focus groups, and actively seeking feedback from diverse players. By involving these voices in the development process, games can better reflect the experiences and perspectives of different communities.

Responsible representation also extends to narrative design. Stories in games should explore a variety of themes and experiences, moving beyond the dominant cultural narratives. This can involve telling stories from the perspectives of marginalized groups, addressing social issues, and exploring diverse cultural traditions and histories. Games like "Life is Strange" and "Never Alone" are examples of how games can tell powerful stories that resonate with diverse audiences.

The representation of gender in games is a particularly important aspect of responsible representation. Female characters should be portrayed as strong, capable, and diverse, moving beyond traditional gender roles. This includes avoiding the objectification of female characters and providing them with agency and depth. Games like "Horizon Zero Dawn" and "The Last of Us Part II" have been praised for their strong, complex female protagonists.

Similarly, the representation of LGBTQ+ characters should be handled with care and respect. This involves creating characters whose sexual orientation or gender identity is a part of their character but not the sole defining feature. Positive and nuanced portrayals of LGBTQ+ characters can promote acceptance and understanding, as seen in games like "The Outer Worlds" and "Dream Daddy."

Ethnic and cultural representation also requires careful consideration. Games should celebrate cultural diversity and avoid cultural appropriation. This involves accurately depicting cultural practices, avoiding caricatures, and ensuring that cultural elements are used respectfully and with permission. Games like "Black Panther" and "Ghost of Tsushima" demonstrate how cultural representation can be done thoughtfully and respectfully.

In addition to character and narrative design, responsible representation involves creating inclusive environments. This includes considering the accessibility of games for players with disabilities, offering language options, and designing gameplay mechanics that accommodate different cultural norms and practices. Ensuring that all players can enjoy and participate in games is a fundamental aspect of responsible representation.

In conclusion, responsible representation in games is essential for creating inclusive, respectful, and engaging gaming experiences. It involves avoiding stereotypes, representing a wide range of identities, consulting with communities, and telling diverse stories. By prioritizing responsible representation, developers can create games that resonate with diverse audiences and contribute positively to cultural understanding and social change.

Designing Games with a Purpose

Designing games with a purpose involves creating games that go beyond entertainment to address important social, educational, or ethical issues. These games, often referred to as "serious games," aim to educate, inform, and inspire players, using the power of interactive media to promote positive change. Designing games with a purpose requires a thoughtful and intentional approach, focusing on meaningful content and impactful experiences.

One of the primary goals of purposeful game design is education. Educational games leverage the engaging and interactive nature of games to teach various subjects and skills. For example, games like "Duolingo" use gamification to make language learning fun and effective, while "Foldit" engages players in solving complex scientific problems related to protein folding. These games demonstrate how purposeful design can make learning enjoyable and impactful.

Social impact games address societal issues and aim to raise awareness, promote empathy, and inspire action. These games often tackle themes like poverty, climate change, mental health, and social justice. For instance, "This War of Mine" offers players a harrowing experience of civilian life during wartime, highlighting the human cost of conflict. Similarly, "Sea Hero Quest" is designed to contribute to dementia research by collecting data on spatial navigation.

Ethical games focus on moral decision-making and ethical dilemmas, encouraging players to reflect on their values and choices. These games often present complex scenarios where players must make difficult decisions, exploring the consequences of their actions. Games like "The Walking Dead" series challenge players to navigate moral gray areas, making choices that affect the story and character relationships. These experiences foster critical thinking and ethical awareness.

Games with a purpose also include those designed for health and well-being. These games can promote physical activity, mental health, and overall well-being. For example, "Pokémon GO" encourages players to explore their surroundings and engage in physical activity, while "SuperBetter" is designed to help players build resilience and improve mental health. Purposeful game design in this context involves creating experiences that support and enhance players' health and well-being.

The design process for games with a purpose involves several key considerations. First, developers need to clearly define the purpose and goals of the game. This involves identifying the target audience, the specific issue or topic to be addressed, and the desired outcomes. A well-defined purpose guides the design process and ensures that the game remains focused and impactful.

Second, developers should integrate meaningful content and gameplay mechanics that support the game's purpose. This involves designing challenges, narratives, and interactions that align with the educational, social, or ethical goals of the game. For example, if the game aims to teach environmental conservation, the gameplay mechanics should involve activities like recycling, resource management, and ecosystem restoration.

Third, collaboration with experts and stakeholders is crucial. Developers should work with educators, scientists, social workers, and other experts to ensure that the game's content is accurate, relevant, and impactful. Engaging with the target audience and stakeholders throughout the development process also helps to create a game that resonates with players and achieves its intended purpose.

Fourth, developers should consider the balance between engagement and purpose. While it is important for the game to be educational or impactful, it also needs to be enjoyable and engaging for players. Striking this balance involves designing gameplay that is fun and rewarding, while still conveying the intended messages and achieving the desired outcomes.

Finally, evaluation and iteration are essential in designing games with a purpose. Developers should gather feedback from players and assess the game's impact to ensure that it meets its goals. This involves playtesting, surveys, and data analysis to understand how players interact with the game and what they take away from the experience. Iterative design allows developers to refine and improve the game based on this feedback.

In conclusion, designing games with a purpose involves creating meaningful and impactful experiences that go beyond entertainment. Whether for education, social impact, ethical reflection, or health, these games leverage the power of interactive media to address important issues and promote positive change. By focusing on clear goals, meaningful content, collaboration, engagement, and evaluation, developers can create purposeful games that make a difference in the lives of players and society.

Addressing Addiction and Game Usage

Addressing addiction and game usage involves recognizing the potential for games to become addictive and implementing strategies to mitigate this risk. Game addiction, characterized by excessive and compulsive gaming behavior that interferes with daily life, is a growing concern. Developers have a responsibility to design games in a way that promotes healthy usage patterns and supports players' well-being.

One of the key factors contributing to game addiction is the use of psychological techniques designed to maximize player engagement. These techniques, often referred to as "dark patterns," exploit cognitive biases and reward systems to keep players hooked. Examples include variable reward schedules, where players receive unpredictable rewards, and the fear of missing out (FOMO) induced by limited-time events. While these techniques can increase engagement, they also carry the risk of fostering addictive behaviors.

To address this issue, developers should focus on ethical design practices that prioritize player well-being. This involves creating games that are enjoyable and engaging without relying on manipulative techniques. For instance, developers can implement transparent and fair reward systems, avoiding mechanics that encourage excessive play. Providing players with clear information about the game's mechanics and potential risks also promotes informed and responsible usage.

Another important aspect of addressing game addiction is promoting balance and moderation. Games should be designed to encourage regular breaks and healthy play habits. This can be achieved through features like in-game reminders to take breaks, setting daily playtime limits, and providing tools for players to monitor and manage their gaming habits. Games like "Fortnite" and "World of Warcraft" have implemented such features to support healthier play patterns.

Parental controls and age-appropriate content are also crucial in addressing game addiction among younger players. Developers should provide parents with tools to manage their children's gaming activities, such as setting playtime limits, monitoring in-game purchases, and blocking inappropriate content. Ensuring that games are suitable for the intended age group and include content warnings helps parents make informed decisions about their children's gaming activities.

Education and awareness are key components in addressing game addiction. Developers can collaborate with educators, mental health professionals, and advocacy groups to raise awareness about the potential risks of game addiction and promote healthy gaming habits. This can involve creating educational materials, supporting research on game addiction, and participating in public discussions on the topic.

Support systems for players struggling with game addiction are also important. Developers can provide resources and links to professional help within their games, encouraging players to seek support if needed. Collaboration with mental health organizations and the inclusion of in-game support tools, such as helplines and counseling services, can provide valuable assistance to players facing addiction issues.

Ethical monetization practices are another critical aspect of addressing game addiction. Developers should avoid predatory monetization strategies, such as loot boxes and pay-to-win mechanics, that can exacerbate addictive behaviors. Instead, they can explore alternative revenue models that do not exploit players, such as fair pricing, optional cosmetic items, and subscription services. Transparency in pricing and clear communication about in-game purchases help players make informed decisions.

The role of industry standards and regulations cannot be overlooked in addressing game addiction. Industry organizations and regulatory bodies can establish guidelines and best practices for ethical game design, promoting responsible behavior among developers. Governments and policymakers can also play a role by implementing regulations that protect players, particularly minors, from addictive game mechanics and predatory monetization practices.

In conclusion, addressing addiction and game usage involves a multifaceted approach that includes ethical design practices, promoting balance and moderation, parental controls, education and awareness, support systems, ethical monetization, and industry standards. Developers have a responsibility to create games that are enjoyable and engaging without fostering addictive behaviors. By prioritizing player well-being and adopting responsible practices, the gaming industry can contribute to a healthier and more sustainable gaming environment.

Ethical Considerations in Game Content

Ethical considerations in game content involve ensuring that the themes, narratives, and representations within games are responsible, respectful, and appropriate. As games become a significant cultural medium, developers must consider the impact of their content on players and society. This includes addressing issues such as violence, representation, cultural sensitivity, and social responsibility.

One of the primary ethical considerations in game content is the depiction of violence. While violence is a common element in many games, it is important to consider how it is portrayed and its potential impact on players. Developers should avoid gratuitous violence and ensure that any violent content serves a meaningful purpose within the game's narrative. Research has shown that exposure to violent media can influence attitudes and behaviors, making it crucial to handle such content responsibly.

Representation and inclusivity are also key ethical concerns. Games should strive to represent a diverse range of characters and narratives, avoiding stereotypes and promoting inclusivity. This involves creating characters that reflect different genders, ethnicities, sexual orientations, and abilities in a respectful and accurate manner. Inclusive representation not only enriches the gaming experience but also helps to combat prejudice and promote empathy.

Cultural sensitivity is another important ethical consideration. Games often incorporate elements from different cultures, and it is essential to depict these elements accurately and respectfully. Developers should engage with cultural experts and communities to ensure that their portrayals are authentic and free from stereotypes. This involves understanding the cultural context and avoiding appropriation, where cultural elements are used without proper respect or understanding.

Ethical considerations also extend to the themes and narratives within games. Developers should be mindful of the messages and values conveyed through their games. This includes avoiding content that could be offensive or harmful, such as hate speech, discrimination, and exploitation. Games should promote positive values and respect for all cultures and identities, fostering an environment of inclusivity and understanding.

The portrayal of sensitive topics, such as mental health, trauma, and addiction, requires particular care. These topics should be handled with sensitivity and accuracy, avoiding stigmatization and sensationalism. Consulting with experts and affected communities can help ensure that these portrayals are respectful and supportive. Games like "Hellblade: Senua's Sacrifice," which explores mental health issues with input from psychologists and individuals with lived experience, demonstrate how sensitive topics can be handled ethically.

The ethical implications of game mechanics and design choices are also important. For instance, the use of loot boxes and microtransactions has been widely criticized for encouraging gambling-like behavior, particularly among young players. Developers should consider the potential harm of these mechanics and explore alternative monetization strategies that do not exploit players. Transparency and fairness in game design are essential to maintaining player trust and well-being.

Privacy and data security are critical ethical considerations in the digital age. Games often collect and process personal data from players, making it imperative to handle this information responsibly. Developers should implement robust data protection measures and ensure that players are informed about how their data is used. Respecting players' privacy and obtaining their consent for data collection are fundamental ethical obligations.

The social impact of games is another important ethical consideration. Games have the power to influence attitudes and behaviors, making it crucial to consider their potential effects on society. Developers should aim to create games that promote positive values, such as cooperation, empathy, and critical thinking. Games can also be used as tools for education and social change, addressing important issues like climate change, mental health, and social justice.

In conclusion, ethical considerations in game content are essential for creating responsible, respectful, and impactful gaming experiences. This involves addressing issues of violence, representation, cultural sensitivity, themes, game mechanics, privacy, and social impact. By prioritizing ethical standards, developers can create games that not only entertain but also contribute positively to society. This commitment to ethical content ultimately benefits players, developers, and the broader cultural landscape.

Chapter 17: The Role of Criticism and Analysis

Game Reviews and Critiques

Game reviews and critiques are essential components of the gaming industry. They serve as the primary means by which players and developers receive feedback on games. Reviews can influence purchasing decisions, shape public perception, and guide future development efforts. The importance of game reviews cannot be overstated, as they provide a platform for both praise and constructive criticism.

Critiques often delve deeper than surface-level reviews, examining the intricacies of gameplay mechanics, narrative structure, and artistic elements. They provide an in-depth analysis of a game's strengths and weaknesses, offering valuable insights to developers and players alike. For instance, a critique might explore how a game's mechanics align with its narrative, or how its visual design enhances the overall player experience.

Professional reviewers typically follow a structured approach, evaluating games based on various criteria such as graphics, sound, gameplay, and story. This standardized method ensures consistency and fairness in reviews, allowing for meaningful comparisons between different titles. Additionally, some reviewers may focus on specific genres or aspects of games, providing specialized insights that general reviews might overlook.

User reviews, on the other hand, offer a more personal perspective. They reflect the diverse experiences and preferences of the gaming community, often highlighting issues that professional reviewers might miss. User reviews can also provide a broader range of opinions, making them a valuable resource for potential buyers seeking varied perspectives.

The rise of online platforms and social media has significantly amplified the reach and impact of game reviews. Websites like Metacritic aggregate scores from multiple reviewers, providing an overall rating that many players use as a benchmark. Social media platforms allow for real-time feedback and discussions, fostering a more interactive and engaged community.

However, the influence of reviews and critiques is not without its challenges. Review bombing, where users intentionally give low ratings to a game to express dissatisfaction with unrelated issues, can distort a game's overall rating. Similarly, biased reviews, whether overly positive or negative, can mislead players and undermine the credibility of the review process.

Developers can benefit greatly from paying attention to reviews and critiques. Constructive feedback can highlight areas for improvement and inspire new ideas for future projects. Engaging with the community through responses to reviews can also build goodwill and demonstrate a commitment to quality and player satisfaction.

In conclusion, game reviews and critiques play a crucial role in the gaming industry. They provide essential feedback to developers, inform players' purchasing decisions, and contribute to the ongoing dialogue about what makes a game successful. By understanding and valuing the insights offered through reviews, both developers and players can contribute to a more vibrant and innovative gaming landscape.

Academic Approaches to Game Studies

Academic approaches to game studies offer a unique perspective on the analysis and understanding of video games. These approaches draw from various disciplines, including psychology, sociology, cultural studies, and media theory, to explore the complex interactions between games, players, and society.

One prominent academic framework is ludology, which focuses on the mechanics and structures of games. Ludologists analyze the rules, systems, and gameplay dynamics that define a game, seeking to understand how these elements create meaningful experiences for players. This approach often involves detailed examinations of game design principles, player behavior, and the cognitive processes involved in gameplay.

Narratology, on the other hand, emphasizes the storytelling aspects of games. Narratologists study how games construct narratives, develop characters, and engage players through storytelling techniques. This approach considers games as narrative mediums, comparing them to traditional forms of storytelling such as literature and film. By analyzing the narrative structures and themes within games, narratologists gain insights into how games convey meaning and evoke emotional responses.

Cultural studies approaches to game studies examine the broader social and cultural contexts in which games are created and played. These approaches consider how games reflect, shape, and are influenced by cultural norms, values, and ideologies. Researchers might explore issues such as representation, diversity, and inclusivity in games, or analyze the impact of games on identity formation and social relationships.

Psychological approaches to game studies investigate the cognitive and emotional processes involved in gameplay. Psychologists study how games affect players' attention, memory, problem-solving skills, and emotional states. They also explore topics such as motivation, engagement, and the psychological effects of game design choices. By understanding the psychological underpinnings of gameplay, researchers can inform the design of more engaging and effective games.

Sociological approaches focus on the social dynamics and communities that emerge around games. Sociologists study how players interact within and outside of games, examining topics such as multiplayer dynamics, online communities, and the social implications of gaming practices. This approach also considers the role of games in socialization, communication, and the formation of social networks.

Critical theory approaches to game studies challenge dominant paradigms and seek to uncover underlying power structures and inequalities within the gaming industry and culture. Critical theorists analyze how games perpetuate or challenge social hierarchies, stereotypes, and injustices. They advocate for more inclusive and equitable gaming practices, emphasizing the importance of social justice in game design and analysis.

In conclusion, academic approaches to game studies provide valuable insights into the multifaceted nature of games. By drawing on diverse disciplinary perspectives, researchers can deepen our understanding of how games function, how they affect players, and how they fit into broader social and cultural contexts. These academic insights can inform the development of more thoughtful, inclusive, and impactful games, ultimately enriching the gaming experience for all players.

The Importance of Feedback Loops

Feedback loops are a fundamental concept in game design, playing a crucial role in shaping player experiences and maintaining engagement. A feedback loop refers to the process by which a game responds to player actions, providing feedback that influences subsequent player behavior. Effective feedback loops create a sense of progression, reward, and challenge, essential for a compelling gameplay experience.

Positive feedback loops reinforce successful player actions, rewarding them with in-game benefits such as points, items, or new abilities. These rewards encourage players to continue performing the actions that led to the positive outcomes. For example, in a role-playing game (RPG), defeating enemies might grant experience points, leading to level-ups and increased character strength. This positive reinforcement motivates players to keep engaging with the game's combat mechanics.

Negative feedback loops, on the other hand, introduce challenges or penalties in response to certain player actions, aiming to balance the gameplay and prevent any single strategy from becoming too dominant. For instance, if a player becomes too powerful in a strategy game, the game might increase the difficulty of enemies or reduce resource availability, forcing the player to adapt their strategy. Negative feedback loops ensure that the game remains challenging and engaging, preventing monotony.

Dynamic difficulty adjustment (DDA) is a technique that uses feedback loops to tailor the game's difficulty to the player's skill level. By monitoring player performance and adjusting the game's challenges accordingly, DDA creates a more personalized and enjoyable experience. For example, if a player is struggling with a particular level, the game might reduce enemy strength or provide additional resources to help them progress. Conversely, if a player is excelling, the game might introduce tougher enemies or more complex puzzles to maintain a sense of challenge.

Feedback loops are also essential in multiplayer games, where player interactions and behaviors can significantly impact the game environment. In online games, feedback mechanisms can include leaderboards, rankings, and social features that encourage competition and cooperation. These systems create a dynamic and evolving gameplay experience, where player actions continuously shape the game's social landscape.

Designing effective feedback loops requires careful consideration of timing, frequency, and clarity. Immediate feedback is often more impactful, as it directly connects the player's action with the game's response. However, delayed feedback can also be powerful, creating anticipation and long-term engagement. The frequency of feedback should strike a balance between providing enough reinforcement to guide player behavior and avoiding overwhelming the player with constant updates.

Clarity is crucial in feedback loops, ensuring that players understand the consequences of their actions. Clear visual, auditory, and textual cues help players make informed decisions and adjust their strategies accordingly. For example, a health bar that visibly decreases when taking damage provides clear feedback on the player's status, prompting them to seek health-restoring items or adopt a more defensive playstyle.

In conclusion, feedback loops are a cornerstone of effective game design. They create a dynamic interplay between player actions and game responses, fostering engagement, challenge, and satisfaction. By understanding and implementing well-designed feedback loops, game developers can create more immersive and enjoyable experiences that keep players coming back for more.

Balancing Artistic Vision and Player Expectations

Balancing artistic vision and player expectations is a delicate and often challenging aspect of game development. Developers must navigate the tension between creating a unique, innovative experience that reflects their creative goals and delivering a game that meets the desires and expectations of their audience.

Artistic vision refers to the developer's creative intentions and the unique elements they wish to incorporate into their game. This can include the game's visual style, narrative themes, gameplay mechanics, and overall aesthetic. A strong artistic vision can set a game apart from others, offering players a distinctive and memorable experience. For example, indie games like "Journey" and "Hades" are celebrated for their unique artistic approaches, which contribute significantly to their critical and commercial success.

Player expectations, on the other hand, are shaped by various factors, including genre conventions, marketing, and prior gaming experiences. Players often have preconceived notions about what a game should offer based on these influences. Failing to meet these expectations can result in disappointment and negative reception, even if the game excels in other areas.

To achieve a balance, developers must first understand their target audience. Conducting market research, analyzing player feedback, and studying successful games within the same genre can provide valuable insights into player preferences and expectations. This information can help developers identify which aspects of their artistic vision are likely to resonate with players and which might require adjustment.

Communication is another critical factor in balancing artistic vision and player expectations. Clear and honest communication about the game's features, themes, and intended experience can help manage player expectations. Trailers, developer diaries, and social media updates can provide players with a better understanding of what to expect, reducing the risk of misaligned expectations.

Flexibility and iteration are also essential. While a strong artistic vision is important, being open to feedback and willing to make adjustments can enhance the game's overall quality. Playtesting is a valuable tool in this process, allowing developers to gather player feedback and identify areas where the game may not align with player expectations. Iterating on the game's design based on this feedback can lead to a more refined and satisfying experience.

It's also important to recognize that not all player expectations need to be met. Sometimes, challenging player expectations can lead to innovative and groundbreaking experiences. Games like "Dark Souls" defy conventional design principles, offering a punishing difficulty that many players have come to appreciate. By staying true to their artistic vision, developers can create niche experiences that attract dedicated fanbases.

Ultimately, the goal is to find a balance that allows the game's artistic vision to shine while delivering an experience that resonates with players. This balance can lead to a game that is both creatively fulfilling for the developers and enjoyable for the audience. By carefully considering player expectations and remaining adaptable, developers can create games that stand out in a crowded market and leave a lasting impact on players.

Learning from Criticism

Criticism is an invaluable resource for game developers, providing insights and perspectives that can drive improvement and innovation. Embracing criticism, whether from professional reviewers, players, or peers, is essential for the continuous growth and success of any game development project.

Constructive criticism helps identify areas where a game may fall short, offering specific suggestions for improvement. For example, feedback on gameplay mechanics, narrative elements, or user interface design can highlight issues that developers might not have noticed during development. By addressing these concerns, developers can enhance the overall quality and player experience of their game.

One effective way to learn from criticism is through playtesting. Inviting players to test the game during various stages of development allows developers to gather real-time feedback and observe how players interact with the game.

This process can reveal pain points, confusing mechanics, or unexpected player behaviors. Incorporating this feedback into iterative design cycles ensures that the game evolves in response to player needs and preferences.

Professional reviews and critiques also offer valuable insights. While it can be challenging to read negative reviews, they often provide detailed analyses of a game's strengths and weaknesses. For example, a review might praise a game's art style but criticize its pacing or difficulty curve. By taking these critiques seriously, developers can make informed decisions about which aspects of the game need refinement.

Community feedback is another crucial source of criticism. Engaging with the player community through forums, social media, and feedback forms can provide a wealth of information about player experiences and expectations. Developers can use this feedback to identify common themes and recurring issues, prioritizing areas that need attention. Active engagement with the community also demonstrates a commitment to player satisfaction, fostering goodwill and loyalty.

Learning from criticism requires a mindset of openness and humility. It's important for developers to separate personal feelings from professional feedback, recognizing that criticism is not a reflection of their worth but an opportunity for growth. Encouraging a culture of constructive feedback within development teams can also promote continuous improvement and innovation.

In addition to addressing specific issues, criticism can inspire new ideas and approaches. For example, feedback on a game's narrative might lead to the exploration of different storytelling techniques or character development strategies. Criticism of gameplay mechanics might prompt the integration of new features or the refinement of existing ones. By viewing criticism as a catalyst for creativity, developers can turn challenges into opportunities.

Moreover, sharing lessons learned from criticism with the broader development community can contribute to collective growth. Writing postmortems, giving talks at industry conferences, or participating in panel discussions allows developers to share their experiences and insights. This exchange of knowledge benefits the entire industry, helping developers avoid common pitfalls and adopt best practices.

In conclusion, learning from criticism is a vital aspect of game development. By embracing feedback from various sources and incorporating it into the development process, developers can create more polished, engaging, and successful games. Cultivating a positive attitude toward criticism and fostering a culture of continuous improvement will ultimately lead to better games and a more vibrant gaming industry.

Chapter 18: Game Development Teams and Leadership

Structuring a Game Development Team

Structuring a game development team effectively is crucial for the success of any game project. The composition and organization of the team can significantly impact the development process, collaboration, and the final product. A well-structured team ensures that all aspects of the game are adequately addressed, from design and programming to art and marketing.

A typical game development team consists of several key roles, each with specific responsibilities:

1. **Project Manager**: The project manager oversees the entire development process, ensuring that the project stays on schedule, within budget, and meets quality standards. They coordinate communication between team members, manage resources, and resolve any issues that arise.

2. **Game Designer**: Game designers are responsible for conceptualizing the game's mechanics, story, and overall experience. They create design documents, define gameplay systems, and work closely with other team members to bring their vision to life.

3. **Programmers**: Programmers write the code that makes the game function. They implement gameplay mechanics, develop the game engine, and ensure that the game runs smoothly on various platforms. Different programmers may specialize in areas such as gameplay, graphics, or network programming.

4. **Artists**: Artists create the visual elements of the game, including character models, environments, textures, and animations. They work in various disciplines such as concept art, 3D modeling, and animation to bring the game's world to life.

5. **Sound Designers**: Sound designers are responsible for the game's audio, including music, sound effects, and voice acting. They create

and integrate audio assets that enhance the player's immersion and experience.

6. **Writers**: Writers develop the game's narrative, dialogue, and lore. They work closely with game designers to ensure that the story aligns with the gameplay and overall vision of the game.

7. **Quality Assurance (QA) Testers**: QA testers play a critical role in identifying bugs, glitches, and other issues. They rigorously test the game to ensure it meets quality standards and provide feedback to developers for improvements.

8. **Marketing and PR**: The marketing and PR team is responsible for promoting the game, managing public relations, and engaging with the community. They develop marketing strategies, create promotional materials, and handle communications with players and the media.

Effective communication and collaboration are essential for a successful game development team. Regular meetings, clear documentation, and collaborative tools can help ensure that all team members are aligned and working towards the same goals. Agile methodologies, such as Scrum or Kanban, are often used in game development to facilitate iterative progress and adaptability.

It's also important to foster a positive and inclusive team culture. Encouraging open communication, valuing diverse perspectives, and promoting work-life balance can enhance team morale and productivity. Recognizing and celebrating achievements, both big and small, can motivate team members and reinforce a sense of shared purpose.

In conclusion, structuring a game development team involves assembling a diverse group of skilled professionals and fostering a collaborative environment. Clear roles, effective communication, and a positive team culture are key to delivering a successful game project. By carefully organizing the team and promoting a supportive work environment, developers can overcome challenges and create engaging and memorable games.

Leadership in Game Development

Leadership in game development is a critical factor that influences the success of a project. Effective leaders guide their teams through the complex and often challenging process of game creation, ensuring that the project stays on track and meets its objectives. Leadership in this context involves a combination of vision, communication, adaptability, and empathy.

One of the primary responsibilities of a game development leader is to establish and communicate a clear vision for the project. This vision encompasses the game's core concept, design principles, and overall goals. A strong vision provides direction and inspiration for the team, helping to align their efforts and maintain focus. Leaders must articulate this vision effectively, ensuring that every team member understands and embraces it.

Communication is a cornerstone of effective leadership. Leaders must facilitate open and transparent communication within the team, creating an environment where ideas can be shared, feedback is welcomed, and concerns are addressed promptly. Regular meetings, clear documentation, and collaborative tools can support this communication. Leaders should also be approachable and responsive, making themselves available to their team members and addressing issues as they arise.

Adaptability is another essential trait for leaders in game development. The industry is dynamic, with new technologies, trends, and challenges emerging regularly. Leaders must be flexible and open to change, willing to pivot their strategies and approaches when necessary. This adaptability extends to problem-solving, as unexpected obstacles often arise during development. Effective leaders can navigate these challenges with creativity and resilience, keeping the project on course.

Empathy is a crucial component of leadership in game development. Understanding the needs, motivations, and challenges of team members fosters a supportive and collaborative environment. Empathetic leaders listen to their team, acknowledge their contributions, and provide the necessary support to help them succeed. This support can take various forms, such as offering constructive feedback, providing professional development opportunities, or ensuring a healthy work-life balance.

Delegation is also a key aspect of effective leadership. Leaders must recognize the strengths and expertise of their team members and delegate tasks accordingly. Trusting team members with responsibilities not only empowers them but also allows leaders to focus on high-level strategic decisions. Effective delegation involves setting clear expectations, providing the necessary resources, and offering guidance without micromanaging.

Conflict resolution is another important skill for leaders in game development. Conflicts can arise from differences in opinions, misunderstandings, or interpersonal issues. Leaders must address these conflicts promptly and constructively, facilitating open dialogue and finding mutually acceptable solutions. Maintaining a positive and respectful team environment is essential for collaboration and productivity.

In addition to these skills, successful leaders in game development often exhibit a passion for gaming and a deep understanding of the industry. This passion can be a driving force, inspiring the team and fostering a shared enthusiasm for the project. A deep understanding of the industry helps leaders make informed decisions, anticipate trends, and navigate the competitive landscape.

In conclusion, leadership in game development involves a combination of vision, communication, adaptability, empathy, delegation, and conflict resolution. Effective leaders guide their teams through the complexities of game creation, ensuring that the project stays on track and achieves its goals. By fostering a supportive and collaborative environment, leaders can inspire their teams to create innovative and engaging games that resonate with players.

Collaboration and Communication Strategies

Collaboration and communication are fundamental to the success of any game development project. Effective strategies in these areas ensure that team members can work together seamlessly, share ideas, and overcome challenges.

By fostering a collaborative environment and utilizing effective communication techniques, game development teams can enhance productivity and creativity.

One of the most important strategies for promoting collaboration is to establish clear roles and responsibilities. Each team member should understand their specific duties and how their work contributes to the overall project. This clarity helps prevent overlap, reduces confusion, and ensures that all aspects of the game are addressed. Clear roles also facilitate accountability, as team members know what is expected of them and can be held responsible for their contributions.

Regular meetings are essential for maintaining communication and coordination within the team. These meetings can take various forms, such as daily stand-ups, weekly progress updates, or milestone reviews. The purpose of these meetings is to share updates, discuss challenges, and align efforts. Effective meetings are structured, time-efficient, and focused on actionable items. They provide an opportunity for team members to voice their ideas and concerns, fostering a sense of inclusion and engagement.

Collaborative tools and technologies play a crucial role in supporting communication and teamwork. Project management software, such as Trello, Jira, or Asana, helps teams organize tasks, track progress, and manage deadlines. Communication platforms like Slack or Microsoft Teams facilitate real-time discussions and information sharing. Version control systems, such as Git, enable multiple team members to work on the same codebase simultaneously, reducing conflicts and ensuring consistency.

Creating a culture of open communication is vital for collaboration. Team members should feel comfortable sharing their ideas, asking questions, and providing feedback. Encouraging a respectful and inclusive atmosphere helps ensure that all voices are heard and valued. Leaders play a key role in modeling this behavior, demonstrating openness and actively soliciting input from the team.

Cross-disciplinary collaboration is particularly important in game development, where diverse skills and perspectives are needed to create a cohesive product. Designers, programmers, artists, sound designers, and writers must work together harmoniously. Facilitating cross-disciplinary communication involves creating opportunities for team members from different disciplines to interact, share their expertise, and understand each other's challenges and constraints.

Conflict resolution strategies are also essential for maintaining a collaborative environment. Conflicts are natural in any team setting, but how they are handled can significantly impact the team's dynamics. Encouraging open dialogue, focusing on finding common ground, and addressing issues promptly and constructively can help resolve conflicts effectively. Leaders should act as mediators, guiding discussions and ensuring that resolutions are fair and acceptable to all parties involved.

Documentation is another important aspect of collaboration and communication. Maintaining clear and up-to-date documentation ensures that all team members have access to essential information about the project. This documentation can include design documents, technical specifications, meeting notes, and development guidelines. Well-organized documentation reduces misunderstandings, facilitates onboarding of new team members, and serves as a reference throughout the development process.

In conclusion, effective collaboration and communication strategies are critical for the success of game development projects. By establishing clear roles, holding regular meetings, utilizing collaborative tools, fostering an open communication culture, facilitating cross-disciplinary interactions, resolving conflicts constructively, and maintaining thorough documentation, game development teams can work together more efficiently and creatively. These strategies help ensure that the team's efforts are aligned and that the final product is cohesive, innovative, and engaging.

Handling Conflicts and Challenges in Teams

Handling conflicts and challenges within game development teams is a critical aspect of leadership and team management. Conflicts can arise from various sources, such as differences in opinions, work styles, or interpersonal issues.

Addressing these conflicts effectively ensures a healthy team dynamic and maintains productivity. Similarly, navigating challenges such as tight deadlines, technical difficulties, and creative disagreements is essential for the successful completion of a project.

One of the first steps in handling conflicts is to create an environment where team members feel comfortable expressing their concerns. Open communication is key to identifying and resolving conflicts early. Encouraging team members to speak up and share their perspectives helps prevent minor issues from escalating into major problems. Leaders should actively listen to all parties involved, demonstrating empathy and understanding.

When conflicts do arise, it's important to address them promptly and constructively. Avoiding or ignoring conflicts can lead to resentment and further complications. Leaders should facilitate open discussions, allowing each party to explain their viewpoints and concerns. The goal is to find common ground and develop mutually acceptable solutions. This process may involve compromise, where each party makes concessions to reach a resolution.

Mediation can be an effective strategy for resolving conflicts. A neutral third party, such as a team leader or external mediator, can help guide the discussion and ensure that it remains productive. Mediators can provide an objective perspective, helping the parties involved see the issue from different angles and work towards a resolution.

In addition to interpersonal conflicts, game development teams often face technical and creative challenges. Tight deadlines and resource constraints are common in the industry, requiring effective time management and prioritization. Breaking down tasks into smaller, manageable components and setting clear milestones can help the team stay on track. Regular progress reviews and adjustments to the project plan ensure that the team can adapt to changes and unexpected obstacles.

Creative disagreements are another common challenge in game development. Team members may have different visions for the game's design, narrative, or mechanics. While these disagreements can lead to innovative ideas, they can also cause friction. Encouraging a collaborative approach to creativity, where team members build on each other's ideas rather than competing, can help mitigate conflicts. Brainstorming sessions, where all ideas are considered and discussed, can lead to more cohesive and innovative solutions.

Stress and burnout are significant challenges in game development, particularly during crunch periods. Leaders must recognize the signs of burnout and take proactive steps to support their team. This can include promoting work-life balance, encouraging breaks, and providing resources for stress management. Creating a supportive work environment where team members feel valued and understood helps maintain morale and productivity.

Effective leadership is crucial for navigating conflicts and challenges. Leaders should model positive behaviors, such as active listening, empathy, and resilience. They should also provide clear guidance and support, helping the team stay focused and motivated. Recognizing and celebrating successes, both big and small, can boost team morale and reinforce a sense of shared purpose.

In conclusion, handling conflicts and challenges in game development teams requires a proactive and constructive approach. Open communication, prompt conflict resolution, effective mediation, and supportive leadership are key to maintaining a healthy team dynamic. By addressing conflicts and navigating challenges effectively, teams can stay focused, motivated, and productive, ultimately leading to the successful completion of their game projects.

Building a Successful Game Development Culture

Building a successful game development culture is essential for fostering innovation, collaboration, and overall team satisfaction. A positive and inclusive culture not only enhances productivity but also attracts and retains top talent. Developing such a culture involves intentional efforts to create an environment where team members feel valued, supported, and motivated to contribute their best work.

One of the foundational elements of a successful game development culture is a clear and inspiring vision. This vision should articulate the team's goals, values, and aspirations. It serves as a guiding light, helping team members understand the purpose of their work and how it contributes to the broader mission. Leaders play a crucial role in communicating and reinforcing this vision, ensuring that it resonates with everyone on the team.

Inclusivity and diversity are critical components of a positive culture. Embracing diverse perspectives and backgrounds fosters creativity and innovation. It allows the team to draw from a wide range of experiences and ideas, leading to more well-rounded and engaging games. Leaders should actively promote diversity by creating an inclusive environment where all team members feel welcome and respected. This includes implementing fair hiring practices, providing diversity training, and encouraging open dialogue about inclusivity.

Collaboration and teamwork are at the heart of a successful game development culture. Encouraging a collaborative approach, where team members work together towards common goals, enhances creativity and problem-solving. Creating opportunities for cross-disciplinary collaboration, such as joint brainstorming sessions or integrated project teams, helps break down silos and fosters a sense of unity. Celebrating collaborative achievements reinforces the value of teamwork and collective success.

Transparency and open communication are essential for building trust and cohesion within the team. Leaders should foster an environment where information is shared openly, and team members feel comfortable voicing their ideas and concerns. Regular updates on project progress, challenges, and decisions help keep everyone informed and aligned. Providing avenues for anonymous feedback can also ensure that all voices are heard.

Professional development and growth opportunities contribute to a positive culture by demonstrating a commitment to team members' career advancement. Offering training programs, mentorship, and opportunities to attend industry events helps team members enhance their skills and stay current with industry trends. Supporting continuous learning not only benefits individual growth but also brings new knowledge and capabilities to the team.

Recognition and appreciation are powerful motivators. Acknowledging and celebrating individual and team achievements boosts morale and reinforces a sense of accomplishment. This recognition can take various forms, such as awards, public acknowledgments, or small gestures of appreciation. Leaders should make it a priority to regularly recognize the hard work and contributions of their team members.

Work-life balance is crucial for maintaining long-term productivity and well-being. Game development can be demanding, and periods of crunch time can lead to burnout if not managed properly. Leaders should promote a healthy work-life balance by encouraging regular breaks, setting realistic deadlines, and respecting personal time. Providing flexible work arrangements and support for mental health and well-being further demonstrates a commitment to team members' overall health.

In conclusion, building a successful game development culture requires intentional efforts to create an inclusive, collaborative, and supportive environment. Clear vision, inclusivity, teamwork, transparency, professional development, recognition, and work-life balance are key components of such a culture. By fostering these elements, leaders can create a positive and motivating atmosphere that drives innovation, attracts top talent, and leads to the creation of outstanding games.

Chapter 19: Innovation in Game Development

The Need for Innovation in Games

Innovation is the lifeblood of the gaming industry. It drives the creation of new experiences, pushing the boundaries of what games can be and how they are played. Without innovation, the industry would stagnate, offering only recycled ideas and uninspired gameplay. The need for innovation is more critical than ever as players' expectations evolve and technology advances.

In the early days of gaming, innovation often meant simply making games more visually appealing or complex. Today, it encompasses a wide range of aspects, from narrative and mechanics to player interaction and monetization. Innovative games often become trendsetters, influencing future titles and establishing new genres or sub-genres.

One of the key areas where innovation is needed is in game mechanics. Developers are constantly exploring new ways to engage players, whether through unique control schemes, interactive environments, or AI-driven narratives. These innovations can lead to entirely new gameplay experiences that captivate audiences.

Another critical area is narrative innovation. Traditional storytelling methods are being challenged by interactive narratives, where player choices directly impact the story's outcome. This not only enhances replayability but also allows for more personalized and immersive experiences.

Technology also plays a significant role in driving innovation. The advent of virtual reality (VR) and augmented reality (AR) has opened up new possibilities for game design. These technologies provide immersive experiences that were previously unimaginable, allowing players to step into virtual worlds and interact with them in real-time.

Moreover, innovation is not limited to gameplay and technology. It also extends to the business models used in the industry. The rise of free-to-play games with in-game purchases has revolutionized how games are monetized. This model has proven highly successful, leading to widespread adoption across various genres.

However, innovation comes with its challenges. It requires significant investment in research and development, as well as a willingness to take risks. Not all innovations will be successful, and developers must be prepared to learn from failures and iterate on their ideas.

Collaboration is another essential factor in fostering innovation. Developers, designers, artists, and writers must work together to create cohesive and groundbreaking experiences. This collaborative approach often leads to the most successful and innovative games.

To remain competitive, studios must also stay attuned to industry trends and player feedback. Understanding what players want and how they interact with games can provide valuable insights that drive innovation. This can involve analyzing player data, conducting surveys, and engaging with the gaming community.

Furthermore, the gaming industry can benefit from looking outside its own sphere for inspiration. Innovations in other fields, such as film, music, and technology, can be adapted and integrated into game design. Cross-industry collaboration can lead to unique and groundbreaking experiences.

In conclusion, innovation is essential for the continued growth and evolution of the gaming industry. It enhances player experiences, drives technological advancement, and creates new opportunities for monetization. By embracing innovation, developers can ensure that the gaming industry remains vibrant and dynamic.

Breaking Conventional Game Design Norms

Breaking conventional game design norms is a crucial aspect of innovation in the gaming industry. It involves challenging established ideas and experimenting with new concepts that can redefine the player experience. This process requires creativity, boldness, and a willingness to take risks.

One way to break conventional norms is by subverting traditional genre expectations. For example, blending elements from different genres can create unique gameplay experiences. Games like "The Legend of Zelda: Breath of the Wild" combine open-world exploration with action-adventure mechanics, offering a fresh take on both genres.

Another approach is to experiment with non-linear storytelling. Traditional games often follow a linear progression, guiding players through a predefined path. By allowing players to influence the story through their choices, developers can create more immersive and personalized narratives. Games like "The Witcher 3: Wild Hunt" and "Detroit: Become Human" excel in this area, offering branching storylines based on player decisions.

Innovative control schemes can also break conventional design norms. For instance, motion controls and touch screens have introduced new ways to interact with games. The Nintendo Wii popularized motion controls, while mobile games leverage touch interfaces to offer unique gameplay experiences. These innovations have expanded the demographic reach of gaming, attracting new players who may not have engaged with traditional control schemes.

Additionally, procedural generation is a technique that can create diverse and unpredictable game worlds. Instead of manually designing every aspect of a game, developers use algorithms to generate content dynamically. This approach can result in endless replayability and unique experiences for each player. Games like "Minecraft" and "No Man's Sky" showcase the potential of procedural generation.

Breaking norms also involves rethinking game objectives and rewards. Traditional games often focus on winning or achieving high scores. However, games that prioritize exploration, creativity, or emotional experiences can offer more profound and fulfilling gameplay. Titles like "Journey" and "Stardew Valley" emphasize personal growth and discovery rather than competition.

Furthermore, social and multiplayer experiences can be innovated by fostering cooperation and community building. Games like "Among Us" and "Animal Crossing: New Horizons" have become cultural phenomena by encouraging players to collaborate and interact in creative ways. These games demonstrate that social interaction can be a core gameplay element rather than just an add-on.

Another aspect of breaking norms is the integration of real-world elements into games. Augmented reality (AR) games like "Pokémon GO" blend virtual and physical worlds, creating immersive experiences that extend beyond the screen. This approach encourages players to explore their surroundings and engage with the game in new and exciting ways.

Moreover, accessibility is an area where conventional norms can be challenged. By designing games with inclusivity in mind, developers can reach a broader audience. This includes considering players with disabilities and providing options for different skill levels. Games like "Celeste" and "The Last of Us Part II" have been praised for their accessibility features.

Breaking norms also involves questioning the role of violence in games. While many games rely on combat and conflict, there is room for non-violent alternatives that focus on problem-solving, creativity, and empathy. Games like "Animal Crossing" and "Portal" demonstrate that engaging gameplay can be achieved without violence.

In conclusion, breaking conventional game design norms is essential for fostering innovation and keeping the gaming industry dynamic. By challenging established ideas and experimenting with new concepts, developers can create unique and memorable experiences that resonate with players. This approach requires creativity, boldness, and a willingness to take risks, but the rewards are well worth the effort.

Innovative Use of Technology in Games

The innovative use of technology is a cornerstone of modern game development. As technology continues to evolve, it opens up new possibilities for creating immersive and engaging experiences. Developers who leverage these advancements can set their games apart and push the boundaries of what is possible in interactive entertainment.

One of the most significant technological innovations in recent years is virtual reality (VR). VR technology immerses players in a fully interactive 3D environment, providing a sense of presence and realism that traditional screens cannot match. Games like "Half-Life: Alyx" and "Beat Saber" showcase the potential of VR to create unique and captivating experiences.

Augmented reality (AR) is another transformative technology. AR overlays digital elements onto the real world, blending physical and virtual experiences. "Pokémon GO" is a prime example of how AR can turn everyday environments into interactive game spaces, encouraging players to explore their surroundings and interact with virtual objects.

Artificial intelligence (AI) is also playing a crucial role in innovation. Advanced AI techniques can create more realistic and responsive non-player characters (NPCs), enhancing the overall gameplay experience. AI-driven characters that learn and adapt to player behavior can provide more challenging and dynamic interactions. Games like "The Last of Us Part II" utilize AI to create lifelike NPCs that react intelligently to the player's actions.

Procedural generation is a technique that uses algorithms to create game content dynamically. This approach can generate vast and varied game worlds, offering endless replayability. "No Man's Sky" is an example of a game that uses procedural generation to create an entire universe of unique planets, each with its own ecosystems and challenges.

Cloud gaming is another technological innovation that is changing the landscape of the industry. By leveraging cloud computing, games can be streamed directly to devices without the need for powerful hardware. This makes high-quality gaming experiences more accessible to a broader audience. Services like Google Stadia and NVIDIA GeForce NOW are leading the charge in this area.

Blockchain technology is also making its way into the gaming industry. Blockchain can provide secure and transparent transactions, making it ideal for in-game economies and virtual goods. It also enables the creation of unique digital assets, such as non-fungible tokens (NFTs), which players can own, trade, and sell. Games like "Axie Infinity" are exploring the potential of blockchain to create player-driven economies.

Additionally, advancements in graphics technology continue to push the visual boundaries of games. Real-time ray tracing, for instance, allows for more realistic lighting and reflections, creating visually stunning environments. Games like "Cyberpunk 2077" and "Control" utilize ray tracing to enhance their graphical fidelity.

Another area of technological innovation is haptic feedback. Advanced haptic technologies can provide tactile sensations, making interactions in games more immersive. The PlayStation 5's DualSense controller, for example, offers haptic feedback and adaptive triggers that simulate the feeling of different textures and resistances.

Furthermore, the use of big data and analytics is transforming game development. By analyzing player data, developers can gain insights into player behavior, preferences, and engagement. This information can be used to fine-tune game mechanics, balance difficulty, and create personalized experiences. Games as a service (GaaS) models often rely on data analytics to continuously improve and update the game based on player feedback.

Finally, the integration of voice recognition and natural language processing (NLP) technologies is enabling more interactive and intuitive gameplay. Players can use voice commands to interact with game characters or control the game, adding a new layer of immersion. Games like "The Elder Scrolls V: Skyrim" with voice-activated mods demonstrate the potential of these technologies.

In conclusion, the innovative use of technology in games is driving the industry forward, creating new opportunities for immersive and engaging experiences. By embracing advancements in VR, AR, AI, procedural generation, cloud gaming, blockchain, graphics, haptic feedback, big data, and voice recognition, developers can push the boundaries of what is possible in interactive entertainment.

Pushing Narrative Boundaries

Pushing narrative boundaries is essential for creating compelling and memorable gaming experiences. As players seek deeper and more meaningful stories, developers must explore new ways to tell narratives that resonate on an emotional and intellectual level. This involves experimenting with narrative structures, themes, and interactive elements to create stories that stand out.

One way to push narrative boundaries is by exploring non-linear storytelling. Traditional narratives follow a linear progression, guiding players through a predefined path. Non-linear narratives, however, allow players to influence the story through their choices, leading to multiple endings and varied experiences. Games like "The Witcher 3: Wild Hunt" and "Detroit: Become Human" excel in this area, offering branching storylines that change based on player decisions.

Another approach is to incorporate meta-narratives, where the game acknowledges its own existence as a game. This can create unique and thought-provoking experiences that challenge players' perceptions. "Undertale" and "The Stanley Parable" are examples of games that use meta-narratives to engage players in unconventional ways.

Interactive narratives are also pushing boundaries by giving players more agency in the story. Rather than being passive recipients of the plot, players become active participants who shape the narrative. This can be achieved through dialogue choices, moral decisions, and branching storylines. Games like "Mass Effect" and "Life is Strange" demonstrate the power of interactive storytelling.

In addition to structure, developers are experimenting with themes and subject matter. Games can tackle complex and sensitive topics such as mental health, identity, and social issues, providing players with meaningful and thought-provoking experiences. "Hellblade: Senua's Sacrifice" and "Celeste" are notable examples of games that address mental health in a profound and empathetic manner.

Furthermore, the integration of procedural storytelling is opening new possibilities for dynamic narratives. Procedural storytelling uses algorithms to generate story elements on the fly, creating unique narratives for each playthrough. This approach can result in personalized and unpredictable stories that keep players engaged. "AI Dungeon" and "Shadow of Mordor" utilize procedural storytelling to create adaptive and evolving narratives.

The use of transmedia storytelling is another way to push narrative boundaries. Transmedia storytelling involves telling a single story across multiple platforms, such as games, books, movies, and comics. This creates a richer and more immersive narrative universe. The "Halo" franchise is a prime example, with its story extending across games, novels, and animated series.

Narrative innovation also extends to character development. Creating complex and relatable characters can enhance the emotional impact of the story. Games like "The Last of Us Part II" and "Red Dead Redemption 2" are praised for their deep character development, which makes the narrative more engaging and immersive.

Moreover, the use of voice acting and performance capture is revolutionizing game narratives. High-quality voice acting and realistic character animations bring stories to life, making interactions more believable and emotionally resonant. "God of War" and "L.A. Noire" showcase the potential of performance capture to create cinematic storytelling in games.

Additionally, the integration of real-world elements and current events into game narratives can create timely and relevant stories. Games that address contemporary issues or draw inspiration from real-world events can resonate more deeply with players. "Watch Dogs: Legion" and "The Division 2" incorporate real-world themes into their narratives, adding a layer of realism and relevance.

Lastly, collaborative storytelling, where players contribute to the narrative, is an emerging trend. Games that allow players to create and share their own stories foster a sense of community and creativity. "Dreams" and "Minecraft" are platforms where players can craft their own narratives, blurring the line between player and creator.

In conclusion, pushing narrative boundaries is crucial for creating engaging and memorable gaming experiences. By exploring non-linear storytelling, interactive narratives, complex themes, procedural storytelling, transmedia storytelling, character development, performance capture, real-world elements, and collaborative storytelling, developers can craft stories that resonate deeply with players.

Future Trends and Opportunities in Game Design

The future of game design is filled with exciting trends and opportunities that promise to reshape the industry. As technology continues to advance and player preferences evolve, developers must stay ahead of these trends to create innovative and engaging experiences. Here are some key trends and opportunities that will shape the future of game design.

One major trend is the continued growth of virtual reality (VR) and augmented reality (AR). These technologies provide immersive experiences that allow players to interact with digital environments in new ways. The development of more affordable and accessible VR and AR hardware will likely lead to wider adoption and new opportunities for game design. Games like "Half-Life: Alyx" and "Pokémon GO" have already demonstrated the potential of these technologies.

Another trend is the rise of cloud gaming. By leveraging cloud technology, games can be streamed directly to devices without the need for powerful hardware. This makes high-quality gaming experiences more accessible to a broader audience. Services like Google Stadia, Microsoft xCloud, and NVIDIA GeForce NOW are leading the charge in this area. Cloud gaming also opens up possibilities for seamless cross-platform play and persistent game worlds.

Artificial intelligence (AI) will continue to play a significant role in the future of game design. Advanced AI techniques can create more realistic and responsive non-player characters (NPCs), procedural content generation, and adaptive gameplay experiences. AI-driven game design can lead to more dynamic and personalized experiences for players. Games like "The Last of Us Part II" and "Middle-earth: Shadow of Mordor" showcase the potential of AI in creating lifelike NPCs and adaptive narratives.

The integration of blockchain technology is another emerging trend. Blockchain can provide secure and transparent transactions, making it ideal for in-game economies and virtual goods. It also enables the creation of unique digital assets, such as non-fungible tokens (NFTs), which players can own, trade, and sell. Blockchain-based games like "Axie Infinity" are exploring the potential of decentralized game economies.

Cross-platform play is becoming increasingly important in the gaming industry. Allowing players to interact and compete across different platforms enhances the gaming experience and fosters larger player communities. Developers must design games with cross-platform compatibility in mind to stay competitive. Games like "Fortnite" and "Rocket League" have successfully implemented cross-platform play, setting a precedent for future titles.

Another opportunity lies in the expansion of games as a service (GaaS) models. GaaS involves continuously updating and expanding games with new content, events, and features. This model keeps players engaged over the long term and provides a steady revenue stream for developers. Games like "Destiny 2" and "Apex Legends" have thrived under the GaaS model, offering ongoing content and updates to keep players invested.

The use of big data and analytics will continue to influence game design. By analyzing player data, developers can gain insights into player behavior, preferences, and engagement. This information can be used to fine-tune game mechanics, balance difficulty, and create personalized experiences. Data-driven design allows developers to make informed decisions and create games that resonate with their audience.

Inclusivity and accessibility will also be key considerations in future game design. Designing games that are inclusive and accessible to a wider range of players, including those with disabilities, is essential for reaching broader audiences. Implementing features such as customizable controls, subtitles, and colorblind modes can make games more accessible. Games like "The Last of Us Part II" and "Celeste" have set high standards for accessibility in game design.

Additionally, the fusion of gaming with other forms of entertainment, such as movies and music, presents new opportunities. Interactive storytelling experiences that blend elements of games and other media can create unique and engaging experiences. Projects like "Bandersnatch" on Netflix and "Quantum Break" have explored the potential of interactive entertainment.

Finally, the emphasis on environmental sustainability and ethical considerations will shape the future of game design. As the industry grows, developers must consider the environmental impact of game development and adopt sustainable practices. Ethical considerations, such as avoiding exploitative monetization practices and promoting positive social values, will also be important.

In conclusion, the future of game design is filled with exciting trends and opportunities. By embracing advancements in VR and AR, cloud gaming, AI, blockchain, cross-platform play, GaaS models, big data, inclusivity, interactive entertainment, and sustainability, developers can create innovative and engaging experiences that resonate with players.

Chapter 20: The Future of Game Development

Emerging Trends and Technologies

The future of game development is set to be shaped by a host of emerging trends and technologies that promise to revolutionize the industry. As technology continues to evolve, developers are presented with new tools and opportunities to create more immersive, engaging, and innovative games. Here are some of the key trends and technologies that will define the future of game development.

One of the most significant emerging trends is the rise of virtual reality (VR) and augmented reality (AR). These technologies offer new ways to create immersive gaming experiences that transport players into entirely different worlds. VR provides a fully immersive experience by surrounding the player with a 3D environment, while AR overlays digital elements onto the real world. As VR and AR hardware becomes more affordable and accessible, we can expect to see a wider adoption of these technologies in gaming.

Cloud gaming is another trend that is poised to transform the industry. By leveraging cloud technology, games can be streamed directly to devices without the need for powerful hardware. This makes high-quality gaming experiences more accessible to a broader audience. Cloud gaming services like Google Stadia, Microsoft xCloud, and NVIDIA GeForce NOW are already making waves, and their impact is expected to grow in the coming years.

Artificial intelligence (AI) is also playing a crucial role in the future of game development. Advanced AI techniques can be used to create more realistic and responsive non-player characters (NPCs), dynamic game environments, and personalized gameplay experiences. AI-driven game design allows for more adaptive and intelligent behavior, making games more engaging and challenging. Games like "The Last of Us Part II" and "Middle-earth: Shadow of Mordor" have demonstrated the potential of AI in creating lifelike NPCs and adaptive narratives.

Blockchain technology is emerging as a game-changer for in-game economies and virtual goods. Blockchain provides a secure and transparent way to manage transactions and digital assets, enabling the creation of unique items that players can own, trade, and sell. Non-fungible tokens (NFTs) are a prime example of how blockchain is being integrated into games, allowing for the creation of one-of-a-kind digital collectibles. Games like "Axie Infinity" are exploring the potential of decentralized game economies powered by blockchain.

Cross-platform play is becoming increasingly important in the gaming industry. Allowing players to interact and compete across different platforms enhances the gaming experience and fosters larger player communities. Developers are designing games with cross-platform compatibility in mind to meet the growing demand for interconnected gaming experiences. Titles like "Fortnite" and "Rocket League" have set a precedent for cross-platform play, and this trend is expected to continue.

Games as a service (GaaS) is a model that involves continuously updating and expanding games with new content, events, and features. This approach keeps players engaged over the long term and provides a steady revenue stream for developers. Successful GaaS titles like "Destiny 2" and "Apex Legends" demonstrate the potential of this model to create lasting player engagement. As the industry moves forward, more developers are likely to adopt the GaaS approach.

Big data and analytics are also playing a significant role in shaping the future of game development. By analyzing player data, developers can gain valuable insights into player behavior, preferences, and engagement. This information can be used to fine-tune game mechanics, balance difficulty, and create personalized experiences. Data-driven design allows developers to make informed decisions and create games that resonate with their audience.

Inclusivity and accessibility are becoming key considerations in game development. Designing games that are inclusive and accessible to a wider range of players, including those with disabilities, is essential for reaching broader audiences. Implementing features such as customizable controls, subtitles, and colorblind modes can make games more accessible. Games like "The Last of Us Part II" and "Celeste" have set high standards for accessibility in game design.

Interactive storytelling is another area with immense potential. Blending elements of games and other forms of entertainment, such as movies and music, can create unique and engaging experiences. Projects like "Bandersnatch" on Netflix and "Quantum Break" have explored the potential of interactive storytelling, offering players the ability to influence the narrative through their choices.

Finally, the emphasis on environmental sustainability and ethical considerations will shape the future of game development. As the industry grows, developers must consider the environmental impact of game development and adopt sustainable practices. Ethical considerations, such as avoiding exploitative monetization practices and promoting positive social values, will also be important for the industry's future.

In conclusion, the future of game development is set to be shaped by emerging trends and technologies such as VR, AR, cloud gaming, AI, blockchain, cross-platform play, GaaS, big data, inclusivity, interactive storytelling, and sustainability. By embracing these trends and technologies, developers can create innovative and engaging games that resonate with players and push the boundaries of what is possible in interactive entertainment.

The Next Generation of Game Developers

The next generation of game developers is poised to drive the industry forward with fresh ideas, innovative approaches, and a diverse set of skills. As the gaming landscape continues to evolve, these new developers will play a crucial role in shaping the future of game design and development. Here are some key factors that will define the next generation of game developers.

Education and training are becoming increasingly important for aspiring game developers. Many universities and colleges now offer specialized programs in game design, development, and related fields. These programs provide students with the technical skills, creative knowledge, and industry insights needed to succeed in the gaming industry. Additionally, online courses and resources are making game development education more accessible to a wider audience.

Diversity and inclusion are also critical considerations for the future of game development. The industry is recognizing the importance of having diverse voices and perspectives in the development process. This diversity can lead to more inclusive and representative games that resonate with a broader audience. Efforts to promote diversity in game development, such as initiatives and scholarships for underrepresented groups, are helping to create a more inclusive industry.

Collaboration and interdisciplinary work are becoming essential for modern game development. The complexity of contemporary games often requires expertise from various fields, including art, music, writing, psychology, and computer science. The next generation of game developers will need to work effectively in interdisciplinary teams, leveraging the strengths of each team member to create cohesive and innovative games.

The rise of indie game development is another significant trend. Independent developers are making a substantial impact on the industry by creating unique and experimental games that may not fit the traditional mold. The success of indie titles like "Hades," "Celeste," and "Hollow Knight" demonstrates that there is a strong market for innovative and creative games developed by small teams. The accessibility of game development tools and digital distribution platforms has empowered indie developers to bring their visions to life.

Technological proficiency will be a key skill for the next generation of game developers. As technology continues to advance, developers must stay updated with the latest tools, engines, and programming languages. Proficiency in engines like Unity and Unreal Engine, as well as knowledge of programming languages such as C++ and Python, will be essential for creating high-quality games. Additionally, understanding emerging technologies like VR, AR, and AI will give developers a competitive edge.

Community engagement and player feedback are becoming integral to the development process. The next generation of game developers will need to actively engage with their player communities, gather feedback, and iterate on their designs based on player input. This iterative approach ensures that games are continually refined and improved, leading to better player experiences. Platforms like Discord, Reddit, and social media provide valuable channels for developers to connect with their communities.

Ethical considerations will play a more prominent role in game development. The next generation of developers will need to navigate issues such as data privacy, microtransactions, and representation responsibly. Creating games that promote positive social values and avoid exploitative practices will be crucial for maintaining player trust and fostering a healthy gaming ecosystem.

Sustainability is another important consideration for future game developers. As the industry grows, developers must consider the environmental impact of game development and adopt sustainable practices. This includes optimizing resource usage, reducing energy consumption, and exploring eco-friendly distribution methods. Sustainable game development practices will help minimize the industry's environmental footprint.

Globalization is expanding the reach of the gaming industry, creating opportunities for developers worldwide. The next generation of game developers will need to consider cultural differences and preferences when designing games for a global audience. Localization and cultural sensitivity will be essential for creating games that resonate with players from different regions and backgrounds.

In conclusion, the next generation of game developers will shape the future of the gaming industry with their fresh ideas, diverse perspectives, and innovative approaches. By focusing on education, diversity, collaboration, technological proficiency, community engagement, ethical considerations, sustainability, and globalization, these developers will create games that push the boundaries of interactive entertainment and resonate with players worldwide.

Predictions for the Future Game Market

Predicting the future of the game market involves analyzing current trends, technological advancements, and consumer behavior. As the gaming industry continues to grow and evolve, several key predictions can be made about the future game market. Here are some insights into what the future may hold for the gaming industry.

One significant prediction is the continued growth of the gaming market. The global gaming industry has been experiencing rapid expansion, and this trend is expected to continue. The increasing accessibility of gaming through mobile devices, cloud gaming, and affordable consoles will contribute to a broader audience and higher revenue. According to market research, the gaming industry is projected to reach new heights in terms of market size and revenue in the coming years.

Mobile gaming will remain a dominant force in the market. With the proliferation of smartphones and tablets, mobile games have become incredibly popular. The convenience of playing games on-the-go and the availability of free-to-play titles with in-app purchases have driven the growth of mobile gaming. Developers will continue to focus on creating engaging and monetizable mobile experiences to capture this lucrative market segment.

Cloud gaming is poised to revolutionize the industry. By leveraging cloud technology, games can be streamed directly to devices without the need for powerful hardware. This makes high-quality gaming experiences more accessible to a broader audience. As internet infrastructure improves and latency issues are addressed, cloud gaming is expected to gain widespread adoption. Services like Google Stadia, Microsoft xCloud, and NVIDIA GeForce NOW are at the forefront of this trend.

Virtual reality (VR) and augmented reality (AR) will continue to evolve and expand. These technologies offer immersive experiences that transport players into entirely new worlds. As VR and AR hardware becomes more affordable and user-friendly, we can expect to see a wider adoption of these technologies in gaming. Developers will create more sophisticated and compelling VR and AR experiences, further enhancing the appeal of these platforms.

The integration of artificial intelligence (AI) will transform game development and player experiences. Advanced AI techniques can create more realistic and responsive non-player characters (NPCs), dynamic game environments, and personalized gameplay experiences. AI-driven game design will lead to more adaptive and intelligent behavior, making games more engaging and challenging. The use of AI in procedural content generation and game balancing will also become more prevalent.

Blockchain technology will play a significant role in shaping the future game market. Blockchain provides a secure and transparent way to manage transactions and digital assets, enabling the creation of unique items that players can own, trade, and sell. Non-fungible tokens (NFTs) are a prime example of how blockchain is being integrated into games, allowing for the creation of one-of-a-kind digital collectibles. Blockchain-based games like "Axie Infinity" are exploring the potential of decentralized game economies.

Cross-platform play will become increasingly important. Allowing players to interact and compete across different platforms enhances the gaming experience and fosters larger player communities. Developers will design games with cross-platform compatibility in mind to meet the growing demand for interconnected gaming experiences. This trend will lead to more seamless and inclusive gaming environments.

Games as a service (GaaS) will continue to thrive. The GaaS model involves continuously updating and expanding games with new content, events, and features. This approach keeps players engaged over the long term and provides a steady revenue stream for developers. Successful GaaS titles like "Destiny 2" and "Apex Legends" demonstrate the potential of this model to create lasting player engagement. More developers will adopt the GaaS approach to maintain player interest and generate ongoing revenue.

Inclusivity and accessibility will be key considerations for future game development. Designing games that are inclusive and accessible to a wider range of players, including those with disabilities, is essential for reaching broader audiences. Implementing features such as customizable controls, subtitles, and colorblind modes can make games more accessible. The industry will continue to prioritize inclusivity to create games that resonate with diverse player groups.

The fusion of gaming with other forms of entertainment will create new opportunities. Interactive storytelling experiences that blend elements of games, movies, and music can offer unique and engaging experiences. Projects like "Bandersnatch" on Netflix and "Quantum Break" have explored the potential of interactive entertainment, and this trend is expected to continue. The convergence of different media forms will lead to innovative and immersive experiences.

In conclusion, the future game market will be shaped by the continued growth of the industry, the dominance of mobile gaming, the rise of cloud gaming, advancements in VR and AR, the integration of AI and blockchain, the importance of cross-platform play, the success of GaaS models, the emphasis on inclusivity and accessibility, and the fusion of gaming with other forms of entertainment. By staying ahead of these trends and leveraging new technologies, developers can create engaging and innovative experiences that resonate with players worldwide.

The Role of VR and AR in Future Games

Virtual reality (VR) and augmented reality (AR) are set to play a transformative role in the future of gaming. These technologies offer immersive and interactive experiences that go beyond traditional gaming, creating new possibilities for gameplay, storytelling, and player engagement. Here are some key insights into the role of VR and AR in future games.

VR technology immerses players in a fully interactive 3D environment, providing a sense of presence and realism that traditional screens cannot match. Players can explore virtual worlds, interact with objects, and experience gameplay from a first-person perspective. As VR hardware becomes more affordable and accessible, we can expect to see wider adoption of this technology in gaming.

One of the key advantages of VR is its ability to create immersive experiences that transport players to entirely different worlds. Games like "Half-Life: Alyx" and "Beat Saber" demonstrate the potential of VR to create unique and captivating experiences. The sense of presence and interactivity in VR games can lead to more intense and engaging gameplay.

AR technology, on the other hand, overlays digital elements onto the real world, blending physical and virtual experiences. AR games like "Pokémon GO" have shown how this technology can turn everyday environments into interactive game spaces. By encouraging players to explore their surroundings and interact with virtual objects, AR games create a unique blend of reality and fantasy.

The role of VR and AR in future games extends beyond entertainment. These technologies have the potential to revolutionize education, training, and therapy. VR simulations can provide realistic training environments for various professions, from medical procedures to military exercises. AR applications can enhance educational experiences by overlaying digital information onto real-world objects, making learning more interactive and engaging.

In terms of gameplay, VR and AR can offer new mechanics and interactions that are not possible with traditional gaming. VR allows for natural and intuitive interactions, such as reaching out to grab objects or physically moving to dodge obstacles. AR can create location-based gameplay that encourages players to explore their surroundings and interact with real-world elements. These new mechanics can lead to innovative and exciting gameplay experiences.

Social interactions in VR and AR are also poised to become more significant. Virtual social spaces where players can meet, interact, and collaborate are becoming increasingly popular. Platforms like VRChat and Rec Room provide virtual environments where players can socialize, play games, and create content together. The sense of presence and immersion in these virtual social spaces can lead to more meaningful and engaging interactions.

Furthermore, the integration of VR and AR with other technologies can enhance the gaming experience. Combining VR with haptic feedback can provide tactile sensations, making interactions in games more immersive. The use of AI in VR and AR can create more dynamic and responsive environments, where NPCs react intelligently to player actions. These integrations can push the boundaries of what is possible in gaming.

One of the challenges for VR and AR in gaming is ensuring comfort and accessibility. Motion sickness and discomfort can be issues for some players in VR, and developers must design experiences that minimize these effects. Accessibility features, such as customizable controls and options for different play styles, are essential to make VR and AR games inclusive for all players.

Another challenge is creating content that fully utilizes the potential of VR and AR. Developing high-quality VR and AR games requires a different approach to design and development, focusing on immersion, interactivity, and player experience. As the industry gains more experience with these technologies, we can expect to see more innovative and polished VR and AR games.

In conclusion, VR and AR are set to play a transformative role in the future of gaming. By creating immersive and interactive experiences, these technologies offer new possibilities for gameplay, storytelling, and player engagement. As VR and AR hardware becomes more accessible and developers gain more experience with these technologies, we can expect to see a wider adoption and more innovative uses of VR and AR in gaming.

Preparing for the Evolving Game Industry

The game industry is constantly evolving, driven by technological advancements, changing consumer preferences, and emerging trends. Preparing for this evolving landscape requires developers, publishers, and stakeholders to stay informed, adapt to new challenges, and embrace opportunities for innovation. Here are some key strategies for preparing for the future of the game industry.

Staying informed about industry trends and technological advancements is crucial. The gaming industry is highly dynamic, with new technologies and trends emerging regularly. Developers should keep up-to-date with the latest developments in areas such as virtual reality (VR), augmented reality (AR), artificial intelligence (AI), blockchain, and cloud gaming. Attending industry conferences, participating in online forums, and following industry publications can help developers stay informed and gain insights into future trends.

Investing in continuous learning and skill development is essential for staying competitive in the evolving game industry. As new technologies and tools emerge, developers must acquire new skills and expertise to leverage these advancements. Online courses, workshops, and training programs can provide valuable opportunities for skill development. Encouraging a culture of continuous learning within development teams can ensure that they remain adaptable and proficient in using new technologies.

Embracing diversity and inclusion is vital for fostering innovation and creativity. Diverse teams bring different perspectives and ideas to the table, leading to more inclusive and representative games. Developers should prioritize diversity in hiring practices and create an inclusive work environment where all team members feel valued and empowered. This approach can lead to games that resonate with a broader audience and reflect a wide range of experiences and cultures.

Collaborating with other industries and disciplines can lead to innovative and groundbreaking experiences. Game development often intersects with fields such as film, music, education, and healthcare. Collaborative projects that combine expertise from different disciplines can result in unique and compelling games. For example, working with educators to create educational games or partnering with healthcare professionals to develop therapeutic VR experiences can open up new opportunities.

Prioritizing player feedback and community engagement is essential for creating successful games. Engaging with the player community through social media, forums, and playtesting can provide valuable insights into player preferences, issues, and suggestions. Developers should actively seek feedback and iterate on their designs based on player input. Building a strong and supportive community around a game can also enhance player loyalty and long-term engagement.

Focusing on ethical considerations and responsible game design is crucial for maintaining player trust and fostering a positive gaming ecosystem. Developers should consider the ethical implications of their design choices, such as data privacy, monetization practices, and representation. Avoiding exploitative practices and promoting positive social values can lead to a healthier and more sustainable gaming industry. Transparency and open communication with players can also build trust and credibility.

Adopting sustainable practices in game development can minimize the environmental impact of the industry. This includes optimizing resource usage, reducing energy consumption, and exploring eco-friendly distribution methods. Developers can also consider digital distribution and cloud gaming as more sustainable alternatives to physical media. By adopting sustainable practices, the gaming industry can contribute to environmental conservation and reduce its carbon footprint.

Exploring new business models and revenue streams can provide financial stability and growth opportunities. The rise of games as a service (GaaS), subscription models, and in-game purchases has diversified revenue streams in the industry. Developers should experiment with different monetization strategies to find the most effective approach for their games. Providing ongoing content updates, events, and features can also keep players engaged and generate steady revenue.

Preparing for the evolving game industry also involves anticipating and adapting to regulatory changes. The gaming industry is subject to various regulations related to data privacy, content rating, and online interactions. Developers should stay informed about regulatory developments and ensure that their games comply with relevant laws and standards. Proactively addressing regulatory requirements can prevent legal issues and enhance the reputation of the developer.

In conclusion, preparing for the evolving game industry requires staying informed about trends and technologies, investing in continuous learning, embracing diversity and inclusion, collaborating with other industries, prioritizing player feedback, focusing on ethical considerations, adopting sustainable practices, exploring new business models, and anticipating regulatory changes. By implementing these strategies, developers can navigate the dynamic landscape of the gaming industry and create innovative and successful games.

www.ingramcontent.com/pod-product-compliance
Lightning Source LLC
Chambersburg PA
CBHW060912140726
47996CB00001B/223